POEMS FROM DIFFERENT CULTURES

AN ANTHOLOGY

NOTES BY PAUL PASCOE

 Longman

 York Press

The right of Paul Pascoe to be identified as Author of this Work
has been asserted by him in accordance with the
Copyright, Designs and Patents Act 1988

YORK PRESS
322 Old Brompton Road, London SW5 9JH

PEARSON EDUCATION LIMITED
Edinburgh Gate, Harlow,
Essex CM20 2JE, United Kingdom
Associated companies, branches and representatives throughout the world

First published 2003
Sixth impression 2005

10 9 8 7 6

ISBN-10: 0-582-77262-1
ISBN-13: 978-0-582-77262-5

Designed by Michelle Cannatella
Illustrated by Susan Scott
Typeset by Land & Unwin (Data Sciences), Bugbrooke, Northamptonshire
Produced by Pearson Education Asia Limited, Hong Kong

CONTENTS

PREFACE

York Notes are designed to give you a broader perspective on works of literature studied at GCSE and equivalent levels. With examination requirements changing in the twenty-first century, we have made a number of significant changes to this new series. We continue to help students to reach their own interpretations of the text but York Notes now have important extra-value new features.

You will discover that York Notes are genuinely interactive. The new **Checkpoint** features make sure that you can test your knowledge and broaden your understanding. You will also be directed to excellent websites, books and films where you can follow up ideas for yourself.

The **Resources** section has been updated and an entirely new section has been devoted to how to improve your grade. Careful reading and application of the principles laid out in the Resources section guarantee improved performance.

The **Detailed summaries** include an easy-to-follow skeleton structure of the poem, while the section on **Language and style** has been extended to offer an in-depth discussion of the poet's techniques.

The Contents page shows the structure of this study guide. However, there is no need to read from the beginning to the end as you would with a novel, play or poem. Use the Notes in the way that suits you. Our aim is to help you with your understanding of the poems, not to dictate how you should learn.

Our authors are practising English teachers and examiners who have used their experience to offer a whole range of **Examiner's secrets** – useful hints to encourage exam success.

The General Editor of this series is John Polley, Senior GCSE Examiner and former Head of English at Harrow Way Community School, Andover.

The author of these Notes is Paul Pascoe, who has been a Chief and Principal Examiner in English since 1974. Author of a number of textbooks for Secondary pupils, he was until recently Head of English at Formby High Comprehensive School.

The text used in these Notes is the AQA Anthology for GCSE English/English Literature (Specification A for 2004).

PART ONE

INTRODUCTION

HOW TO STUDY A POEM

A poem differs from a piece of prose writing because it is freer in its structure, and it often contains a deliberate rhyme and/or rhythm. When reading a poem, each of these aspects should be considered:

STRUCTURE: The poet has made conscious choices to organise the poem as it appears on the page. Try to understand the poet's thinking behind:

- The organisation of the lines (e.g. into verses)

- Any repetition of lines or varying lengths of line

- Whether lines are **end-stopped** or whether the sense carries over to the next line

RHYME: Consider the rhyming scheme and ask yourself these questions:

- What, if any, is the rhyming scheme?

- Are the rhymes exact or approximate and for what purpose?

- Do some lines have rhyming words within them and why?

- If there are no rhymes, why does the line end where it does?

RHYTHM: Turn to the rhythm of the poem and listen for:

- Which words are stressed

- Whether there is a pattern of sound which creates a mood

- Whether this mood suits the subject matter

SUBJECT MATTER AND THEME: Just like a novel or a play, a poem has a subject matter and a theme. Once you have identified these, consider why the poet has drawn on that particular subject matter to illustrate an idea or develop the theme.

? DID YOU KNOW?
The word 'poetry' comes from the Greek word *poesis*, meaning 'making' or 'creating'. People have been writing poetry for thousands of years – the earliest we have dates back to about 3000 BC.

SETTING AND BACKGROUND

DIFFERENT CULTURES

Culture is a very difficult idea to tie down as it extends into so many areas of life. Someone once said that if you want to find out about water, don't ask a fish. The point is that we all swim in our own culture but because it is as natural to us as breathing, we are barely aware of it unless we step outside of it and become 'like a fish out of water'.

If you travel abroad, for instance, even to a similar country, you become aware of the way people do things differently there, even if it is only a matter of driving on the other side of the road or riding side-saddle on a motorbike. Even if we cannot put our finger on it, we sense that people in, say, France or Italy have a somewhat different way of thinking and looking at life. The difference between 'them and us' is cultural rather than material (just like all westerners, they have computers, cars, mobile phones, etc.).

 DID YOU KNOW?
In France even young people shake hands when they meet.

As many of the poems in the Anthology suggest, culture is somehow tied up with our sense of identity and our roots. Some people feel this more powerfully than others, especially if they have moved away from their origins. For instance, Grace Nichols is a well-known international writer, now living in England, yet in her two poems represented in the Anthology, she explores the magnetism of her West Indian origins.

Of course, the further you travel from familiar territory, the greater the cultural differences are likely to be. Some of the poems here relate to very different worlds than most of us know at first hand. For example, Denise Levertov's **'What Were They Like?'** challenges our ignorant assumptions about a very distant culture.

However, cultural distance is not necessarily measured by geographical distance. Even within your own country you can find examples of different cultures. For instance, in **'Unrelated Incidents'**, the Scottish poet, Tom Leonard, complains about the dominance of London-based media through the use of standard English and received pronunciation.

In **'Two Scavengers in a Truck, Two Beautiful People in a Mercedes'** the American poet, Lawrence Ferlinghetti, presents us with two pairs of fellow citizens from the same society but who may as well have come from different planets. Sometimes such contrasting lifestyles within a broad common culture are described as 'sub-cultures'.

WHAT ARE THE INGREDIENTS OF CULTURE?

Just as it would be impossible to list every single feature that makes up our physical environment, it is impossible to define everything that contributes to what we call 'culture'. However, there are some factors that play a major part:

- Race
- Nationality
- Language
- Religion
- Education
- Wealth/poverty
- Social behaviour
- Attitudes
- Customs

- Traditions
- Literature
- Music
- Painting
- Entertainment
- Sense of humour
- Politics
- Food
- Dress

These are some of the features that make up a kind of invisible, mental environment that affects and influences us all. Just like our physical environment, it is incredibly varied and may frame our behaviour and outlook. **'Limbo'**, for example, powerfully conveys how African slaves, transported like animals with no possessions whatsoever, cling to the only thing over which they have any kind of ownership – their music.

However, it is important not to make the mistake of over-stressing cultural differences. People from all societies share the same human emotions. Love, for instance, is a universal emotion. At the same time, as we are formed in part by our culture, we are also individual

DID YOU KNOW?
Words can take on different meanings in different parts of the country. If you use the word 'bonny' and you live in the south of England, you probably mean 'plump' but if you live in the north, you mean 'pretty'.

DID YOU KNOW?
There is an opera called *Porgy and Bess* by white American composer George Gershwin that only black artists are allowed to perform on stage.

human beings with our own private thoughts and feelings. In fact, few of the poems in the Anthology have the question of different cultures as their central concern. Even when they do (as in **'Presents from my Aunts in Pakistan'**) the focus is on human feelings.

'Night of the Scorpion' is set in rural India and contains specific references to local customs and attitudes, but its real subject is the universal human emotions of fear and love set against a stifling culture of ignorance, superstition and religion. What 'Night of the Scorpion' also illustrates is that it is impossible to bracket people as simply belonging to a particular culture. Most of the people referred to in the poem are uneducated peasants with traditional beliefs but the father, although part of the same community, is better educated and attempts a more rational, if equally desperate and ineffective, way of treating his wife. It is also worth noting that however passionately the writers represented in the Anthology may feel about their cultural roots, they have become almost detached observers as a result of their education and profession. Most have become international figures and move freely from one culture to another. Consequently, many of the poems deal with the *relationship* of one culture with another, whether on a purely personal level as in Grace Nichols' **'Hurricane Hits England'** or on a political level as in Denise Levertov's **'What Were They Like?'**.

Bearing in mind that the poems may have other concerns than culture alone, the geographical and cultural spread reflected in the Anthology is quite wide ranging:

- African – 'Nothing's Changed', 'Vultures', 'Not My Business', 'Limbo'

- Indian – 'Night of the Scorpion', 'Blessing'

- Anglo/Pakistani – 'Presents from my Aunts in Pakistan'

- Indo/American – 'Search For My Tongue'

- West Indian – 'Love After Love'

- Anglo/West Indian – 'Island Man', 'Hurricane Hits England', 'Half-Caste', 'Love After Love'

- American – 'Two Scavengers in a Truck'
- American/Asian – 'What Were They Like?'
- Scottish – 'Unrelated Incidents'

THE POETS

Many of the poems in the Anthology have a strong personal or autobiographical element, so it is interesting and useful to know something about the author's life and background. For instance, Tatamkhulu Afrika was deeply involved in the struggle against apartheid in South Africa and District Six, which figures in **'Nothing's Changed'**, and holds powerful associations for the poet. It is important to know something of these things because it gives us some insight into *why* the poet wrote his poem and feels so passionately about his subject. However, the background facts do not explain *how* the poem works.

Achebe, Chinua (b. 1930): Vultures

Born and educated in Nigeria, Achebe is primarily known as a novelist, though he also has had a distinguished academic career in both Nigeria and in the USA, as well as publishing poetry.

Afrika, Tatankhulu Ishmael (b. 1920): Nothing's Changed

Afrika's names are the key to his identity; none of them was given to him by his Arab father and Turkish mother. Born in Egypt, he was brought up in South Africa. Working for many years as a copper miner in Namibia, he became very involved in the anti-apartheid movement, even refusing to be classified as 'white'. He now describes himself as an 'Africanist' although he is still aware of his Egyptian roots. He has kept the false name – Tatankhulu Afrika – which he had to use when he was banned from speaking in public. When he became a Muslim he added the name Ishmael.

Agard, John (b. 1949): Half-Caste

Agard was born in Guyana (which was then called British Guyana) and moved to Britain in 1977 to join his father. He himself comes from a racially mixed background; his mother came from Portugal

EXAMINER'S SECRET
The examiners are more interested in what you have to say about the poem than what you know about the poet.

CHECK THE NET
Look up 'apartheid' and find out more about race classification.

DID YOU KNOW?

Dubbing originated in Jamaica when DJs produced recordings of songs with the vocal track removed so they could add their own half-spoken, half-sung words.

and his father from Guyana. He works as a lecturer for the British Council, as well as writing and performing his poetry. He calls himself a 'poetsonian' and is sometimes thought of as a 'dub' poet, someone who recites his poetry to a musical soundtrack.

Alvi, Moniza (b. 1954): Presents from my Aunts in Pakistan

Although she was born in Pakistan, Alvi's family brought her to England when she was a baby and she has never learned the language of her father (her mother is English). As a child she did not have any links with the Asian community in Britain. She was brought up as a Christian, as her Muslim father did not practise his faith, and she was educated in England. However, she has always been very aware of her mixed cultural history, and finally went to Pakistan for the first time in 1993.

Bhatt, Sujata (b. 1956): from Search For My Tongue

Bhatt's life contains a fascinating mixture of languages and places. Born in India, her family moved to the USA, where, having already learned Gujarati and Marathi, she learned English. After her marriage she moved to Germany, where she still lives, though she has also briefly worked in Canada. However, she still thinks of herself as Indian and, as well as writing her own poetry (she started aged eight), she translates Gujarati poetry into English.

CHECK THE NET

Look up 'Gujarati' and the other Indian languages.

Brathwaite, Edward Kamau (b. 1930): Limbo

Brathwaite's life encapsulates the diverse cultural background of many West Indians. Born in Barbados, he won a scholarship to Cambridge, and went on to receive a Ph.D. from Sussex University. He worked in Ghana for a number of years, taught history at the University of the West Indies in Jamaica, and also taught in New York. Possibly to assert his ethnic origins and sense of identity, he has deliberately chosen to use the Kikuyu name given to him when he lived in Africa, rather than the more western 'Edward'.

Dharker, Imtiaz (b. 1954): Blessing

Dharker's life crosses many cultural and religious boundaries. Born in Pakistan, she was a year old when her Muslim family moved to Glasgow, where she was educated. She married an Indian Hindu, against the wishes of her parents (whom she did not see for ten years). Now living in India, she and her family celebrate Hindu, Muslim and Christian festivals! Although English is her first language, she speaks an impressive range of others: Punjabi, Marathi, French and German. As well as a poet, she is also an award-winning documentary film-maker and an exhibited artist.

Ezekial, Nissim (b. 1924): Night of the Scorpion

Many critics regard Ezekial as the first major Indian poet to write in English. He was born in Bombay during the British rule in India, and later became involved in the political struggle for independence. He had a multicultural early education. His family was Jewish, and the school contained a mixture of Muslims, Christians, and Parsis, but he says there was no hostility between the various religious groups. He studied English Literature at London University, and later taught for a while in England before publishing his first volume of poetry in 1952.

CHECK THE NET

Look up 'Ghandi' to find out more about the path to independence in India.

Ferlinghetti, Lawrence (b. 1919): Two Scavengers in a Truck ...

Born in New York, Ferlinghetti had early experience of different cultures. He was sent to France when very young, then, aged five, he had to learn English on his return to the USA. Serving in the Navy during the Second World War, he saw the aftermath of the dropping of atomic bombs on Japan. This led him to become a pacifist. A leading 'beat' poet, he was a publisher, and owned a famous bookshop, City Lights (after a Charlie Chaplin film.) Like the 'cool' man in his poem, he liked expensive cars, driving an Aston Martin.

CHECK THE NET

Look up 'Enola Gay' to find out about the dropping of the first atomic bombs.

Leonard, Tom (b. 1944): **from** *Unrelated Incidents*

Leonard was born in Glasgow. His father is Irish, and his mother Scottish, so he has strong family links with Scotland and has lived there for most of his life, though he did work for a while for the Post Office in London. When he left school, he worked in various jobs, gaining further qualifications part-time. Eventually he was able to attend Glasgow University where he gained his degree.

Levertov, Denise (1923–97): What Were They Like?

Levertov had a very varied cultural background. She had a Welsh mother, a Jewish father who became a Christian minister, and she was born and educated in England but, having lived in the USA since her marriage in 1947, was an American citizen. Educated at home, she wanted to be a writer from the age of six, publishing her first poem aged seventeen. She has published over twenty volumes of poetry, as well as translating Hindu writers. She is also associated with the 'beat' poets, like Ferlinghetti. She was socially and politically active, campaigning against the Vietnam War and nuclear weapons, and supporting the feminist movement.

CHECK THE NET

Look up 'beat poets' to find out more about this style of poetry.

Nichols, Grace (b. 1950): Island Man; Hurricane Hits England

Born in Georgetown in what was then British Guyana, Nichols had a very 'English' education, studying English Literature at university. She worked as a teacher and journalist before settling in England in 1977. She says that she feels at home in both the Caribbean and England, perhaps helped by the fact that she was born by the sea and now lives by the sea in Sussex.

CHECK THE NET

Look up 'Nigerian civil war' to find out more about the background of both Osundare and Achebe.

Osundare, Niyi (b. 1947): Not My Business

Born in Nigeria, but also educated in Britain and Canada, Osundare is very much concerned about African politics and culture. (His own country has suffered a devastating civil war.) A much-respected writer and poet, as well as being a Professor of English at Ibadan University, he was awarded Africa's most important literary prize in 1990. He feels strongly that poetry should be performed as part of an oral tradition, and he himself has travelled all over the world doing this.

DID YOU KNOW?

There is an 'Ig Noble Prize'. In 2001 the prize for Literature was awarded to an Englishman, John Richards, for founding the Apostrophe Protection Society.

Walcott, Derek (b. 1930): Love After Love

Born and educated in the West Indies, Walcott has had a distinguished academic career in both the Caribbean and the USA. The outstanding nature of his poetic achievement was recognised by the award of the Nobel Prize for Literature in 1992. He has also written many successful plays.

PART TWO

SUMMARIES

EDWARD KAMAU BRATHWAITE – Limbo

❶ The silent dark of the slave ship is described.

❷ Someone starts to beat out the rhythm and the speaker of the poem begins to dance.

❸ The speaker squeezes under the stick, rises in triumph and feels a sense of almost trance-like exhilaration.

When you first read the title of this poem, you may have thought of the dance so often seen in tourist pictures, but think carefully about all these other definitions of 'limbo':

- An imaginary place of the lost forgotten or unwanted
- An unknown place between two extremes
- A prison
- The place where, according to the Christian religion, the unbaptised are sent as they cannot enter heaven

(Collins English Dictionary 1999 – millennium edition)

These other meanings would have also been in Brathwaite's mind when he wrote this poem, which is based on the dance reputedly devised by slaves during their transportation from Africa to the Caribbean.

The poem is not constructed as a logical narrative, but attempts to create a sequence of images reflecting the terrible experience of being human cargo on the slave ships.

The unifying factor is the rhythm of the limbo dance and the refrain; 'limbo, limbo like me' runs through the poem. Some kinds of music, including jazz, start off with a group of notes or a simple

DID YOU KNOW?
It is claimed that the limbo stick was originally the iron bar to which the slaves were chained on board ship.

DID YOU KNOW?

Brathwaite himself has performed his poetry. You could try reading this poem aloud, even acting it out with a group of friends. Then you will really hear the rhythm.

tune and then create and develop many variations from it. In a similar way, Brathwaite starts this poem by introducing a number of key words and ideas (lines 1–9). From lines 10 to 37, he reuses, repeats and recombines words and phrases to produce a number of vivid, almost incantatory (chanting) phrases. Take, for example, the words in line 7: 'long, dark night'. We then have a series of variations: 'long dark deck' (twice: lines 16, 17); 'dark deck is slavery' (twice: lines 21, 23); 'dark still steady' (line 13); 'the darkness is over me' (line 27); 'the dark ground is under me' (line 33).

The word 'silence', in the opening line, is also reused in this section; you might like to look through where this happens, and also trace through the poet's use of the word 'stick' (also in line 1).

Many of the key words in this poem are single syllables and have sharp-sounding consonants: 'stick', 'dark', 'deck', 'whip', 'knock', 'drum', 'hit', 'still'. These create a regular beat, like the drum used to accompany the dance; there are very few **polysyllabic** words in the poem.

As the slaves begin to dance, the drum beats out and the rhythm and excitement grow to a climax in lines 34–36, as the dancer goes under the limbo stick.

The drumming has an almost hypnotic effect on the dancer, 'the drummer is calling me' (line 37), and the language of the poem changes at this point. After the repeated references to whips, sticks and the dark horror of the slave hold, we have references to sunrise (often used as a symbol of hope), 'praising' (line 41), and of being lifted up – 'raising me' (line 43). The rhythm here becomes quicker, suggesting excitement, through the use of a cluster of polysyllabic words, and unstressed syllables (see lines 37, 41, 43, and 47). The poet talks of the music 'saving' him (line 47). Through the dance, the speaker triumphs over his suffering and captivity. However, the last four lines remind us that these feelings are likely to be short-lived: his suffering will continue when the ship arrives at its destination and he has to set foot on the 'burning ground' (line 51).

CHECKPOINT 1
What other poem uses sunrise but *not* as a symbol of hope?

Links

Sense of identity
- Island Man
- Search For My Tongue
- Unrelated Incidents
- Half-Caste
- Love After Love
- Presents from my Aunts...
- Hurricane Hits England

Spoken voice
- Unrelated Incidents
- Half-Caste

Repetition
- Night of the Scorpion
- What Were They Like?
- Half-Caste
- Not My Business

Unusual form
- What Were They Like?
- Search For My Tongue
- Unrelated Incidents

 DID YOU KNOW?

In the Middle Ages, people accused of various religious crimes could try to prove their innocence by walking over burning coals and not being harmed. Even today, various Eastern holy men demonstrate their faith by walking on hot coals.

TATAMKHULU AFRIKA – Nothing's Changed

1 The narrator picks his way across the scrubland of District Six.

2 A modern restaurant has been opened, offering expensive food.

3 There is no sign outside as there would have been in the days of apartheid, saying it is for whites only, but black people would not be welcome there.

4 The narrator contrasts the luxury of the restaurant with the lifestyle of local working people.

5 The narrator is angry because nothing has changed.

'Nothing's Changed' is probably the most specifically autobiographical poem in the Anthology. The author, Tatamkhulu Afrika, was deeply involved in the anti-apartheid movement in South Africa and was an active member of the African National Congress (ANC), which since its foundation in 1912 fought for freedom from white minority rule. With the release of Nelson Mandela from captivity in 1990 and free elections in 1994, the dream of a multi-racial state seemed to have come true.

District Six

In this poem, the author examines the effect of the new multi-racial government on an area of Cape Town, known as District Six. District Six had been a bustling, cosmopolitan community until 1966, when the government declared the district to be a 'whites only' area.

The existing population was evacuated and the community destroyed. Tatamkhulu Afrika was one of those who rebelled against the decision and was arrested by the security police. Eventually, in 1982, the area was bulldozed so that no trace of its origins remained. To this day, the area is essentially a wasteland, with just a few attempts to revitalise it, as in the case of the restaurant that figures in the poem.

 CHECK THE NET

For more detailed background information, look up 'Cape Town', 'District Six', 'ANC', 'Nelson Mandela' etc.

One of the poem's most striking features is its rhythm and its extensive use of **monosyllables**. In fact, two thirds of the poem's vocabulary and almost half the lines are monosyllabic. For example, the first line comprises entirely of monosyllables and establishes a sense of a throbbing pulse, a kind of heartbeat, lying below the surface of the whole poem, sometimes fading, at other times beating more loudly. If the poet had written 'Tiny hard stones click', the effect would have been quite different, much lighter and tripping.

The result of this insistent beat is to give all the numerous details in the poem a close up, physical quality as though they are *felt* rather than merely *observed*. The effect is intensified by the poet's use of a compressed grammar with, for instance, no unnecessary connecting words, so that there seems to be no space between the details that crowd in: 'new, up-market, haute cuisine, / guard at the gatepost, / whites only inn' (lines 22–24). This technique is appropriate because the poem is shot through with a simmering anger; the poet makes no pretence at being detached or simply descriptive. Even the opening walk suggests that the ground underfoot, strewn with hard stones and discarded cans, is uncomfortable, unwelcoming and resistant to visitors. Only the 'amiable weeds' (line 8) seem to be at home.

To the outsider the area is anonymous, but too much of the writer's past lives here. He does not need a sign or visual clues; he knows it is District Six in his whole being, in his feet, his hands, his bones, etc. (lines 11–16). The repeated use of the word 'and' hammers home the cumulative effect of his growing anger.

The focus shifts to a new restaurant grotesquely standing among the weeds and the imported Port Jackson 'designer' trees. The poet resents its appearance for it is out of place; it is 'Brash' (line 17) and 'it squats' (line 19). However it is doubly out of place because it is a 'whites only inn' (line 24). In the same way as he does not need a board to help him recognise District Six, he does not need a sign on the restaurant for him to know that he would not be welcome there: 'we know where we belong' (line 26).

At the heart of the poem is a contrast between the cool, purity of the inn with its 'haute cuisine' (line 22) and the 'plastic table's top'

CHECKPOINT 2

What do you think is the significance of the 'clear panes' (line 28) that the speaker presses his nose against?

squalor of the 'working man's café' serving 'bunny chows' (lines 34–37).

Commanding a line to itself, 'the single rose' (line 32), beautifully set off by the linen table cloth, seems to embody the screaming injustice of so much wealth arrogantly displaying itself amongst so much poverty. The problem of a lack of change in attitudes also underlies the reference to how the workmen in the café 'spit a little on the floor' (line 39). The poet **ironically** uses what might be the words of an apartheid supporter, who would argue that the black people are incapable of behaving any better because 'it's in the bone' (line 40) – that's the way they are made. But the whole poem suggests that the poor are still waiting to be released from these deep-seated, restrictive attitudes.

DID YOU KNOW?

In early twentieth-century Britain, some people objected to providing bathrooms in working-class housing because they said the tenants would not know how to use them.

In the final stanza, the poet feels the whole experience is a throwback to a former life – 'boy again' (line 42) – when he raged against the injustice of white rule. The cold, impersonal glass seems as in need of a stone or a bomb to destroy it as the apartheid regime of the past.

The last line echoes the title: 'Nothing's changed'.

Links

Political/social comment

- Two Scavengers...
- Vultures
- What Were They Like?
- Unrelated Incidents
- Not My Business

First person point of view

- Limbo
- Night of the Scorpion
- Search For My Tongue
- Half-Caste
- This Room
- Not My Business

- Presents from my Aunts...
- Hurricane Hits England

Sense of place

- Island Man
- Blessing
- Two Scavengers...
- Night of the Scorpion
- Vultures
- What Were They Like
- Hurricane Hits England

Rich and poor

- Blessing
- Two Scavengers...

CHECKPOINT 3

What has changed and what hasn't changed?

GRACE NICHOLS – Island Man

❶ The man wakes up still hearing in his head the sounds of the sea.

❷ These sounds evoke pictures of early morning on his island.

❸ He hears the real sounds of London traffic which blot out the sounds in his head.

❹ He has to face another day in London.

 CHECK THE NET

Look up BBC Online and Windrush to find out more about immigration from the Caribbean.

In this poem Grace Nichols re-creates the waking thoughts of an unnamed man. He has travelled to London, as many people from the Caribbean have done, to find work, originally at the invitation of the British government. But the implication is that he still yearns for the Caribbean. It seems that he has been dreaming of his island and for a few minutes on waking it is as if he is back there.

Even though he is living in London, the title of the poem 'Island Man' suggests that he still feels very much part of his original home and culture, at least in his dreams. In fact, the whole poem is constructed as a kind of dream sequence in which images and impressions of the Caribbean and the London traffic merge. One technique the poet employs to suggest that the Caribbean lives in his dreams is to use words that blend with one another. An example is when the poet refers to the waves. She makes up the word 'wombing' (line 5) where we might expect to her to use 'booming', which suggests that their rhythm and sound is like the heartbeat a child hears in the womb. This made-up word is less defined than a regular word but also more suggestive – just like a dream. He tries to wake up.

> **CHECKPOINT 4**
>
> Why is 'groggily' repeated and separated from the rest of line 11?

He has to 'heave' himself from 'his crumpled pillow waves' (line 17) and his pleasant thoughts of home. Nichols uses a play on words to show the transition from dreams to waking when she uses the word 'sands' (which he has been thinking of) instead of 'sounds' for the roar of traffic: 'sands of a grey metallic roar' (lines 12–13).

As readers we may sympathise with him. His 'island home' is presented to us by Nichols as idyllic – like the pictures we may have seen of the Caribbean on holiday programmes: the sun rising on a scene of 'blue surf' (line 3), rhythmic booming of the waves, picturesque fishermen, brilliant colours – 'emerald' (line 10) – the sea birds. In contrast, London is presented at its 'dull' (line 15) worst: 'grey' (line 13), harsh sounding – 'metallic' (line 13), 'roar' (line 15) – full of the noise of traffic.

Does the man perhaps subconsciously realise that his vision of the Caribbean is just a little too idyllic? There is no mention of the possible poverty or unemployment that may have caused him to emigrate in the first place.

There is a poignant sense of resignation shown in the three words of the last line, which Nichols has separated out from the rest of the poem: 'Another London day' (line 19).

Links

Sense of identity

- Limbo
- Search For My Tongue
- Unrelated Incidents
- Half-Caste
- Love After Love
- Presents from my Aunts...
- Hurricane Hits England

Sense of place

- Nothing's Changed

- Blessing
- Two Scavengers...
- Night of the Scorpion
- Vultures
- What Were They Like?
- Hurricane Hits England

Rhetorical effects

- Limbo
- Half-Caste
- Hurricane Hits England

IMTIAZ DHARKER – Blessing

1 There is a dire need for water in the unremitting heat.

2 We imagine collecting such water as there is in a tin mug, drip by drip.

3 A water main bursts.

4 People rush to gather what they can in all manner of containers, while the children dance in the sparkling fountain.

For most of us, nothing is more ordinary than water; a burst main is more than likely to be seen as an inconvenience and the phrase 'dying of thirst' no more than a metaphor. But for a huge slice of humanity, water is scarce. Sudden, unexpected abundance is the ultimate good fortune. 'Blessing' captures the essence of this feeling.

The poem is set on the edge of a city, though there is no mention of any specific setting because this situation is repeated in similar places around the world.

 DID YOU KNOW?

The seventeenth century English poet, George Herbert, wrote of 'Heaven in ordinarie'. The phrase seems to sum up the sense of wonder and joy that we sometimes find in simple things, just like the children's excitement about the water.

Blessing continued

DID YOU KNOW?

The immediate setting and the source of the poet's reflection, is the vast shanty town outside Bombay or Mumbai, as it is now known. The settlement has no official status and there is no regular water supply.

The first line confronts us with a stark image of human skin breaking open like a seed pod in the heat; the second is an unambiguous statement, devoid of imagery: 'There never is enough water'.

In the second section the precise image of each drop echoing in an almost empty container emphasises the slow, patient task of gathering even a tiny quantity of water. Even so, the suggestion is of gratitude rather than resentment; the slow dripping in the mug is 'the voice of a kindly god' (line 6).

After this austere opening, the poem explodes into a sequence of glittering, intertwining images of gushing water. Interestingly, after line two, the word 'water' itself does not appear again. Instead, it becomes transformed into 'silver' (line 9) and a 'blessing' (line 22), something precious and divine.

The sound of the 'kindly god' (line 6) has grown from a hollow rattle in a nearly-empty mug to 'a roar of tongues' (line 11) as people chatter and celebrate their good fortune. The people who rush to collect the unexpected gift are a 'congregation' (line 12), as if they are worshippers in a religious building.

The sudden change in the situation is reflected in the form of the poem. As the pipe bursts, clear-cut sentences give way to a more fluid construction built around an extended list of people and containers with several uses of **enjambment** to accentuate the sense of flow.

The poem seems to end positively, with the excited 'screaming' children, the embodiment of innocent joy, at the centre of images of brightness – 'liquid sun', 'polished', 'flashing light' (lines 19–21). Even the children's skin, once dry and cracked, seems jewel-like, 'polished to perfection' (line 20).

But such events happen only 'Sometimes' (line 7). The pipe will be repaired and the sun will once again crack the skin 'like a pod' (line 1). Furthermore, there is a tragic **paradox** at the heart of the situation. The water pipe only passes through their community. The drought is man-made because they have no official access to the water it carries.

Where, we might ask, does the 'municipal pipe' (line 8) lead to? To the city, to official buildings, the homes of the rich, or the luxury hotel in which tourists are staying?

CHECKPOINT 5

Why do you think there are no commas separating 'man woman child' (lines 12–13)?

 CHECK THE NET

Look up the charity 'WaterAid' to find out more.

Links

Sense of place
- Nothing's Changed
- Island Man
- Two Scavengers…
- Night of the Scorpion
- Vultures

- What Were They Like?
- Hurricane Hits England

Rich and poor
- Two Scavengers…
- Nothing's Changed

Now take a break!

LAWRENCE FERLINGHETTI – Two Scavengers in a Truck ...

1 Two couples find themselves side by side at traffic lights.

2 Two garbagemen (bin men) hang on the back of a bin-lorry and look down at a smart couple in an open-top Mercedes.

3 The two couples are contrasted.

4 The poem reminds us of how a democratic society *ought* to unite people of all kinds.

CHECKPOINT 6

Why does Ferlinghetti describe the garbagemen's clothing?

It is perhaps easiest to see cultural difference as a matter of different race or different nationality. In this poem, Ferlinghetti explores the fact that sharp cultural divides exist within a supposedly single society.

The setting is 1960s America. The poem **juxtaposes** two central images, that of the 'grungy' (line 17) men on the garbage truck and the 'elegant couple' (line 9) in the car. These two images form the poem's main structure and are bold in outline and easily visualised.

To construct these images, the poet uses very little in the way of conventional simile or metaphor, apart from the reference to the 'gargoyle Quasimodo' (line 22) and the comparison with watching TV (line 29). Instead, he provides a series of sharp statements about material features. What is more, we can recognise these or similar images from innumerable Hollywood films.

The two couples brought together in this way represent the extremes in society. The couple in the car are rich and display the symbols of material success: foreign car, smart clothes, and a professional job. The couple on the garbage truck, on the other hand, seem to have no obvious possessions. They depend for their livelihood on society's waste; they are 'scavengers' (line 26), not producers.

The basic contrast is very clear and seemingly very simple but a closer reading finds the poet worrying away at his subject with all sorts of hints, wordplay and little **ironies**:

- The couple in the car are 'cool' in two ways: literally, and also by representing a fashionable lifestyle referred to as 'cool' in contemporary slang.

- The title itself seems clear-cut but it is full of ironic value judgments. The word 'scavengers' is used rather matter-of-factly, almost as though it was a job title, and is repeated twice again in the poem. But are these anonymous men truly like vultures, or is that how society labels them? On the other hand, the other couple are 'Beautiful People'. Does their beauty lie in their character or their appearance and lifestyle? One is reminded of the saying that 'beauty is only skin deep'.

- The two bin men are literally 'hanging on' to the back of the truck and 'looking down' on the Mercedes (lines 5–6). We may wonder whether they are hanging on to the bottom rung of society and yet may be morally superior to the beautiful people. The profession of architect may have more social status, but civilised society would collapse without those willing to clear up its rubbish.

 DID YOU KNOW?

Hollywood actor Lon Cheney starred as Quasimodo in a famous black and white film of *The Hunchback of Notre Dame*. To this day, you can buy models of Cheney as the hunchback.

DID YOU KNOW?

This poem is an equivalent in words of the work of pop artists such as Roy Lichtenstein (1923–97) who drew on images from the mass media and presented them in hard-edged primary colours; 'yellow' (line 3) and 'red' (lines 4 and 31) in this poem are primary colours.

CHECKPOINT 7

Why does the poet identify the make of car?

- The 'elegant open Mercedes' and 'the elegant couple' (lines 8–9) are linked in an empty-sounding statement that reflects the superficiality of the couple and of society.

- The 'sunglasses' (line 12) are a fashion accessory and long hair was highly fashionable in the 1960s. But the fact that the younger of the men on the truck was 'also with sunglasses & long hair' (line 24) suggests that the lifestyle aspirations of the two are more closely linked than might at first seem. They are also 'about the same age' (line 25).

- The couple in the car seem to represent the 'American dream' exemplified in TV advertisements where 'all is possible'. But we wonder how possible it would be for the garbagemen to achieve this kind of affluent lifestyle. The older man seems to represent what the future holds for the younger one.

- The world of the TV advertisement is also sanitised – 'odorless' (line 29) – and therefore unreal, in contrast to the work-stained world of 'real' people like the men on the truck.

At the end of the poem the lights change and the two sets of people go their different ways, like ships on 'the high seas' (line 36). Although the poet has invited us to think about connections and links between these people, the final image is of a 'gulf' (line 35) which cannot be bridged. We are back to the two separate elements of the title; notice there is not even an 'and' to connect the two.

Links

Sense of place	Political and social comment
• Nothing's Changed	• Nothing's Changed
• Island Man	• Vultures
• Blessing	• Unrelated Incidents
• Night of the Scorpion	• Half-Caste
• Vultures	• Not My Business
• What Were They Like?	
• Hurricane Hits England	

NISSIM EZEKIEL – Night of the Scorpion

1 The narrator remembers the night when his mother was bitten by a scorpion.

2 Neighbours flocked to the scene chanting prayers and searching for the scorpion.

3 Her husband tried to be logical and attempted to cleanse the bite with burning paraffin.

4 Eventually, the narrator's mother recovered and gave thanks that the scorpion picked her and not one of the children.

In some ways, 'Night of the Scorpion' concerns a clash of cultures within a culture. The setting is rural India. The peasant population is steeped in an age-old culture of religion and legend in which life and death are always closely related. At the same time, there are those who either through education or background have more in common with western ideas than traditional Indian values and beliefs. In this poem, the father a 'sceptic, rationalist' (line 36) is one such person.

CHECKPOINT 8

Do you think that the author is a 'rationalist' like his father?

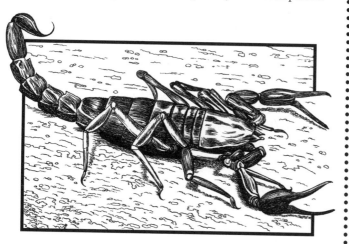

Despite the desperate nature of the situation, the poet acts as a detached observer, noting what happens but making no direct comment. The only clues to the narrator having any connection

Night of the Scorpion continued

with the events are the references to 'my mother' (line 1) and 'My father' (line 36). This method contrasts sharply with the passionate engagement of Tutamkhulu Afrika in **'Nothing's Changed'**. The poem is almost devoid of imagery. There is just a single, rather conventional simile: 'like swarms of flies' (line 8).

However, the poem is more than a dry, matter-of-fact catalogue of events because the poet gives it **rhetorical** and dramatic shape. The opening (lines 1–7), recounting the visit of the scorpion, is quite low-key and self-contained; the scorpion comes, stings and leaves. The poet implies that the creature acted solely in the interests of self-protection and survival. Its tail may seem a thing of the devil – 'diabolic' (line 6) – but in reality, the scorpion left the protection of the rice sack and *it* 'risked the rain again' (line 7) because it was disturbed by humans.

> **CHECKPOINT 9**
>
> In what ways does the poet link the scorpion and the neighbours?

Unlike the opening, the sentence and line patterns in the central section are particularly elaborate and ornate.

The repeated framework 'May . . . they said' (lines 18–29) with its nagging stress on 'they said' is somewhat artificial because the more natural sentence structure is **inverted** ('May he sit still, they said' instead of 'They said, may he sit still').

At the same time, the poet uses variation in sentence and line structure to create a feeling of irregularity within a general flow. For instance, lines 23–26 comprise a single flowing sentence but are broken into four distinct phrases by the line divisions. In this way the poet creates some sense of the chaotic babble in the hut mingling with the continual drone of the prayers.

The onlookers' flow of advice and prayers is of little comfort to the suffering woman, attempting as it does to make a virtue out of the event, which they assume will almost certainly be fatal. The peasants pray that the sting will decrease her suffering in the next life or that her pain may serve to reduce the totality of evil in the world. They even hope that, should she survive, the experience will teach her a lesson and rid her of 'desire' and 'ambition' (line 28).

As they chant, the peasants sit around the woman writhing in agony and wear the look of 'the peace of understanding' (line 31). Here the poet deliberately chooses this conventional religious phrase to suggest that the onlookers are more concerned with their own smug moral satisfaction than actually caring for the woman.

In the final part of this section (lines 36–45), the verse becomes more agitated with shorter, rather more clipped phrases: 'My father, sceptic, rationalist' (line 36), etc. The father desperately tries a more scientific remedy, by attempting to cauterise (cleanse by burning) the wound. At the same time, the holy man continues to perform his ritual chanting. The verse builds to a climax. The words 'I watched' (line 41) first begin a single line sentence, then a weighty double line sentence, (lines 42–43) until the language subsides into a simple, neutral, evenly-stressed statement: 'After twenty hours / it lost its sting' (lines 44–45).

The recovery is a fact. Scorpion stings are not necessarily fatal. Whether the father's treatment or the holy man's prayers had anything to do with it is a matter of interpretation but the narrator offers no opinion; he simply 'watched' (lines 41–42).

All the way through the poem, the mother, the centre of action and comment, suffers in silence. Even the title of the poem seems to focus attention onto the cause of her suffering, rather than onto her. We hear her voice when the danger is past, after twenty hours of pain, and the single statement – 'my mother only said' (line 46) – seems to reinforce her self-effacing concern for her children (for whom the sting would have been much more likely to be fatal).

The poem is particularly interesting because unlike, for example, **'Nothings Changed'**, the poet manages to convey genuine feeling for his mother by being detached rather than openly involved. This contrasts with the over-emotional villagers who do not seem to consider the feelings of the woman herself. By chanting supposed truths about life and death, they show themselves to be blind to the truth. Like Imtiaz Dharker, Ezekial is suspicious of narrow beliefs and cultures. The literal room of 'Night of the Scorpion' contains as much prejudice as Dharker's metaphorical room.

DID YOU KNOW?

There are parallels with the Bible story of Job, who was subjected by God to various afflictions and whose friends (or 'comforters') only made his suffering worse.

EXAMINER'S SECRET

The **Links** boxes suggest which poems may be compared because they touch on similar themes and ideas, but you also need to recognise important differences between them if you are to gain the highest marks.

Links

Contrasting cultures

- Nothing's Changed
- Island Man
- Two Scavengers...
- What Were They Like?
- Search For My Tongue
- Unrelated Incidents
- Presents from my Aunts...
- Not My Business

Human attitudes and relationships

- Two Scavengers...
- Vultures
- What Were They Like?
- Love After Love
- Not My Business

Sense of place

- Nothing's Changed
- Island Man

- Blessing
- Two Scavengers...
- Vultures
- What Were They Like?
- Hurricane Hits England

First person point of view

- Limbo
- Nothing's Changed
- Search For My Tongue
- Half-Caste
- This Room
- Not My Business
- Presents from my Aunts...
- Hurricane Hits England

Repetition etc.

- Limbo
- What Were They Like?
- Half-Caste
- Not My Business

Now take a break!

CHINUA ACHEBE – Vultures

❶ The poet observes a pair of vultures roosting near some carrion.

❷ They cause the poet to think about the unlikely places in which love may be found.

❸ Even in a Nazi concentration camp, there may be acts of affection.

❹ Does this mean that there is some good in every creature, or that those capable of love must also be capable of evil?

Despite its title, this poem is not really about vultures – although the author contemplates them in some detail. Rather, the poem is concerned with good and evil and their place in humanity. Even so, it is these scavenging birds that set the poet thinking.

The poem opens at dawn, often an optimistic prelude to a new beginning. In this case, however, we are presented with uniformly depressing images: the new day is smudged with 'drizzle' and dawn is 'despondent' (line 2). There are no 'harbingers' (line 3), such as birds bursting into song, to greet the new day. Instead the scene is dominated by a vulture and his mate.

The description of the vultures and their behaviour draws upon our disgust at creatures that can live off rotting, dead flesh. The poet's **diction** is full of words with negative associations: 'broken bone', 'dead tree', 'bashed-in', 'dump', 'gross', 'swollen corpse', 'water-logged', 'gorged', 'hollowed remnant', 'cold' (lines 5–20). He skilfully organises the elements in his description to play on certain deep-seated feelings of fear and revulsion. Even though few westerners have ever observed vultures in their natural habitat, there is a kind of universal consciousness that casts these birds, along with creatures such as rats, as the evil side of creation.

Achebe brings together two sets of tactile (to do with touch) associations. First there are number of phrases – 'broken bone', 'smooth bashed-in', 'pebble on a stem', 'telescopic eyes' (lines 5–21) – that are not only grotesque but suggest something cold, hard-edged, devoid of life and feeling, rather like a skeleton. These dry, pitiless

? DID YOU KNOW?
Vultures live almost entirely off carrion.

DID YOU KNOW?

In reality, vultures pair up for life, may live together for forty or fifty years and care for their offspring for up to a year.

GLOSSARY

charnel house a building where bones were deposited

Commandant military commander

images are interspersed with contrasting images of dampness and foul-smelling decay: 'swollen corpse', 'water-logged trench' and possibly 'dump', in the American sense of a word for 'excrement' (lines 11–16). Put the two sets of images together and one has a recipe for horror.

The birds' actual behaviour is no less revolting. We cringe at the thought of eyes being pecked out and the 'things' (line 17) they ate in the corpse's bowels.

However, in the midst of this horror there is a momentary vision of something different and seemingly out of place, but which the whole of the long opening sentence (lines 1–12) leads up to. The male 'inclined affectionately' to his mate.

The poet finds it strange how such love as the vultures seem to exhibit can find a home for itself in a place immersed in death, a 'charnel-house' (line 26), and may even slip into untroubled sleep.

This suggests to the poet a human parallel – the situation of the Belsen concentration camp where the air is full of the stench of burning flesh and the poet's **juxtaposition** of 'human' and 'roast' (line 33) again revolts us, with its suggestion of eating the unspeakable. But the Nazi Commandant brings home chocolate for his children, to whom he is an affectionate 'Daddy' (line 39).

Conclusions?

How does one deal with the question that affection and unspeakable evil can live together in the same creature? The poet offers two answers, neither of which is very comfortable:

❶ We may rejoice that even the most cold-hearted and despicable 'ogre' may harbour some 'tiny glow-worm' of warmth or 'tenderness' (lines 43–45).

❷ Alternatively, we may despair that ultimately love can only exist in the context of eternal evil.

Either way, there seems to be a terrible price to pay for what we call love.

Links

Powerful, central image (s)

- Nothing's Changed
- Blessing
- Love After Love
- This Room

Sense of place

- Nothing's Changed
- Island Man
- Blessing
- Two Scavengers...
- Night of the Scorpion
- What Were They Like?
- Hurricane Hits England

Human attitudes and relationships

- Two Scavengers...
- Night of the Scorpion
- What Were They Like?
- Love After Love
- Not My Business

Political and social comment

- Nothing's Changed
- Two Scavengers...
- What Were They Like?
- Unrelated Incidents
- Not My Business

CHECKPOINT 10

Why is the Commandant referred to as 'Daddy'?

DENISE LEVERTOV – What Were They Like?

❶ The first part of the poem consists of six questions about the people of Vietnam and their way of life.

❷ The second part consists of individual answers to these questions.

At first sight, this may not appear to be a poem at all. The numbered lines have an appearance of a student worksheet relating to some sort of project on the people of Vietnam. The questions are framed in the past tense as though they relate to an ancient civilisation. In fact, the six questions are of the sort that archaeologists might ask in search for clues about a forgotten or extinct civilisation like the Incas or Babylonians:

The facts

1. Stone lanterns are commonly seen in the temples of southeast Asia and China, so it would be of interest to know if the Vietnamese also used them.

2. Most civilisations have ceremonies to welcome the coming of Spring – 'the opening of buds'.

3. 'Quiet laughter' suggests a courteous and civilised way of enjoying yourself.

4. Most civilisations make jewellery out of various materials.

5. Many early societies celebrated their heroes and great deeds in history in so-called epic poems.

6. These poems might be either spoken or sung.

? DID YOU KNOW?

A famous early English poem called *Beowulf* recounts tales of the hero slaying monsters and saving his people.

Of course, the presentation is deliberate. To most Americans, Vietnam was a remote and unknown country. The people of North Vietnam were simply 'the enemy'; essentially faceless and alien, as far removed from American experience as any ancient tribe. But at the same time the Vietnam War was a most painful engagement for the United States. The first American troops were deployed in Vietnam as early as 1950 but official US involvement in fighting was 1961–75. In that time over 200,000 Americans and as many as 1 million Vietnamese were killed during the conflict.

What is less known is that Vietnam is an ancient culture. Its origins are wreathed in legend but the earliest kingdom may date back to nearly 3000 BC. Throughout their long history, the Vietnamese have fought many invaders or colonisers – notably the Chinese and, more recently, the French.

In the second half of the poem an attempt is made to answer the questions. Although the unknown respondent politely addresses the questioner as 'Sir', the focus of the response is not on the 'facts' as requested, but on the human anguish and suffering caused by the war. The speaker picks up a key word or idea in each question and transfers it to what s/he thinks is a more important issue.

The suffering

1. Heavy hearts – 'stone' – rather than picturesque illuminated gardens.

2. The death of young children, not the growth of flowers.

3. Mouths that have been napalmed – 'burned' – cannot laugh.

4. Human bodies have been burned, they have no use for jewellery made of animal bone.

5. The culture and peaceful civilisation which might produce epic stories has been totally destroyed.

6. Singing has been replaced by the silence of death.

The responses are expressed in longer sentences, particularly in 'answers' five and six, as if the speaker is becoming more and more involved. The language also grows more emotional, with many words evoking death and destruction.

This destruction forms a sharp antithesis to the former culture which is portrayed with words such as 'pleasant', 'delight', 'peaceful', 'joy', and 'song'. The fragility of this culture is conveyed in the delicate comparison of their singing to a 'flight of moths'.

A sense of the devastation, even annihilation of a people and culture is conveyed by phases such as 'It is not remembered', 'A dream ago'; the past is only an 'echo' or 'reported' and uncertain: 'perhaps', 'maybe'.

The poem goes full circle and ends with a question 'Who can say?'. This final question is much more profound than the 'questionnaire' type questions at the beginning of the poem. The implication is that the opening questions reveal a total lack of understanding of what happened to the Vietnamese. Indeed it exposes the impossibility of answering those questions; the voices of those whose lives are being discussed are now all 'silent'.

 DID YOU KNOW?

One of the most horrifying news pictures of the Vietnam War was of a young girl running screaming along a road, her body burning.

CHECKPOINT 11

What words suggest death and destruction?

 CHECK THE NET

The 'Vietnam War Internet Project' is among many sites that have lots of interesting pictures and information.

What Were They Like? continued

EXAMINER'S SECRET

You will see that poems listed in **Links** boxes often appear under more than one heading. Remember that poems do not have a single meaning but may be considered from a variety of points of view.

Links

Political and social comment

- Nothing's Changed
- Two Scavengers...
- Vultures
- Unrelated Incidents
- Not My Business

Repetition

- Limbo
- Night of the Scorpion
- Half-Caste
- Not My Business

Sense of place

- Nothing's Changed
- Island Man
- Blessing
- Two Scavengers...
- Night of the Scorpion
- Hurricane Hits England

Unusual form and presentation

- Limbo
- Search For My Tongue
- Unrelated Incidents

Now take a break!

FROM WHICH POEM?

1 silver crashes to the ground

....

2 drum stick knock and the darkness is over me

....

3 also with sunglasses & long hair

....

5 Comes back to sands of a grey metallic soar

....

4 there was time only to scream

....

6 I press my nose to the clear panes

....

7 I watched the flame feeding on my mother.

....

8 a tiny glow-worm tenderness

....

Check your answers on p. 98.

SUJATA BHATT– *from* Search For My Tongue

❶ The poet poses the problem of how to cope with two languages.

❷ The poet complains that her mother tongue (Gujarati) is fading, but she has not fully mastered her new language (English).

❸ Living in a new place causes her first language to 'rot and die'.

❹ In her dreams her mother tongue returns once again.

CHECKPOINT 12

Which other two poets in the Anthology also explore the issues of being part of more than one culture?

This poem is based on the poet's personal experience of moving, as a young child, from India to the United States. Although the poem may have an autobiographical base, its concerns have a wider relevance.

Our language is much more than a means of conveying information. All languages may perform the same basic function but each has its own personality, as it were, and to an extent shapes the way we think and respond to the world. Our language is an intimate part of our culture and identity. At the same time, language must fulfil the needs of a particular society, and one reason the poet finds her native language slipping away is that it may not be well suited to all the specific needs of the western society into which she has moved.

DID YOU KNOW?

The Bible refers to 'speaking in tongues', meaning being inspired by the Holy Spirit to speak in many languages.

The use of the word 'tongue' (line 2) to mean 'language' is a conventional, if now rather dated, metaphor. The poet reawakens the metaphor by making us very conscious of the tongue's *physical*, as well as its abstract, meaning. The tongue is 'in your mouth' (line 4): the tongue can 'rot and die' (line 13); she can 'spit it out' (line 14). Indeed, as the poem develops, the tongue seems to take on a life of its own. It 'grows back'; it 'opens in my mouth' and 'blossoms out of my mouth' (lines 31–38).

Including its use in the title, the word is repeated ten times, so that it becomes a kind of **motif** woven into the poem. In this way the poet creates the sense that her language is much more than an idea but an active participant in a personal drama. Although the poem moves to an emotionally rich conclusion, the opening is comparatively neutral. Rather in the manner of **'Half-Caste'** it engages in an imaginary dialogue about a question (lines 1–2). At this point, the word 'tongue' is used quite conventionally to mean 'language' (including a play on the phrase 'lost my tongue' or not knowing what to say, and 'on the tip of your tongue', or struggling to find the right word).

Until some way into the third sentence, the poet seems to be doing no more than calmly presenting the problem of how to deal with forgetting her native language, while not having complete command of her new language. Obviously speaking them both at once is not an option. The use of the second person address – 'what would you do' (line 3) etc. – suggests a level of detachment, as does the absence of imagery in the opening lines.

Then in line 12 'mother tongue' begins to take on the physical characteristics of something organic. The voice shifts from the second person address to the first person: 'you had to spit it out. / I thought I spit it out' (lines 14–15) and the verbs move into the present tense. Suddenly, everything becomes more personal and immediate.

> ### CHECKPOINT 13
> What are the first words in the poem that compare the poet's tongue to a living thing?

The first section of the poem comes to rest mid-sentence on the word 'dream' (line 16). The word offers two simple possibilities: the first that she literally dreams that she is speaking her mother tongue; or secondly, that she longs to speak it.

Dreams, however, have a deeper significance. They hold within them our deepest memories and desires. Dreams are involuntary; we cannot control them or easily erase what they contain. Consequently, although it may be convenient and practical to adopt the new language and 'spit' (line 14) out the mother tongue, the mind will not let go of something so deep-rooted. As if to underline the involuntary nature of the dream, the sentence is first completed not in English, but in Gujarati. Many of the readers of the poem will, at this stage, also experience something of the poet's problem of two languages as we 'hear' a foreign language which, even though it is written phonetically in western script after the Gujarati script, we do not understand. Lines 31–38 provide an English translation.

> ### CHECKPOINT 14
> What other poem in the Anthology uses the idea of dreams betraying our inner feelings?

DID YOU KNOW?

The celebration of spring, heralding rebirth and new growth, plays a central part in most religions and cultures.

The concluding passage is rich in associations of fertility and re-growth, like spring following a barren winter: 'shoot', 'grows moist', 'opens', 'blossoms'. What is more, in contrast to the uncertainty of the opening with its repeated use of 'what' and 'if', and **conditionals** such as 'would' and 'could', the final sequence makes positive statements using present tense verbs: 'grows', 'opens', 'pushes', 'blossoms'. The extended growth metaphor reverses the feeling of decay conveyed in lines 13–15.

The repetition of the key words, 'grows' and 'opens' binds the whole together and mirrors the repetition in the Gujarati passage.

In this way, the whole poem seems to project a contrast between the *rational* argument about the practical use of a language and the *emotional* pull of the language that is part of one's being.

DID YOU KNOW?

Over forty million people speak Gujarati.

It is also worth observing an important difference between English and minority languages such as Gujarati. English is now a world-wide language and not associated with a particular culture, even place. Gujarati is very widely spoken in India but is still associated with an identifiable culture. The state of Gujarat dates back to the fifth century AD and Hindus recount that Lord Krishna visited the region 3,500 years ago. Furthermore, the music and cuisine of Gujarat are distinct to the region.

Links

Sense of identity

- Limbo
- Island Man
- Unrelated Incidents
- Half-Caste
- Love After Love
- Presents from My Aunts…
- Hurricane Hits England

First person point of view

- Limbo
- Nothing's Changed
- Night of the Scorpion
- Half-Caste

- This Room
- Not My Business
- Presents from my Aunts…
- Hurricane Hits England

Unusual form and presentation

- Limbo
- What Were They Like?
- Unrelated Incidents

Language

- Unrelated Incidents
- Half-Caste

TOM LEONARD– *from* Unrelated Incidents

❶ The six o'clock news is read with a Glaswegian accent.

❷ The associations of accents are considered.

To a large extent, how you speak English depends on where you come from. We are all familiar with regional voices, whether they be Geordie, Scouse, Cornish, Welsh, Brummie or whatever. To these, we could add overseas voices, such as Indian, West Indian, American and so on. In fact, nearly all of us reveal our origins by the way we speak, in our **accent** and our **dialect**.

This poem is based on an everyday event – the reading of the six o'clock news. It does not matter if it is radio or television, though the poet may have been **alluding** to a famous wartime experiment in

 DID YOU KNOW?
The newsreader's voice echoes Leonard's own Glaswegian accent.

DID YOU KNOW?

R.P. is also sometimes called 'BBC English' because for very many years it was the only accent heard on the broadcast media.

radio. Voices with certain kinds of regional accents are often thought of as sounding homely or friendly. A well-known broadcaster, a Yorkshireman called Wilfred Pickles, could speak in both received pronunciation and a Yorkshire accent. The BBC thought that their listeners might find the war news a little less grim if he used his Yorkshire accent, but complaints poured in! People said they did not feel they could believe or rely on the news when it was read like this. As the poet says 'if / a toktaboot / thi trooth / lik wanna yoo / scruff yi / widny thingk / it wuz troo' (lines 15–21). Such is the status of standard English and received pronunciation.

> **Accent** relates to how we actually pronounce words. Everyone has an accent, however they speak or wherever they come from. The accent which is linked to no particular part of the country, and is taught to people learning English as a foreign language is called 'received pronunciation' (R.P.).
>
> **Dialect** refers to particular words, phrases or grammatical forms that people use. Once again, everyone uses a dialect. Even so, one English dialect has acquired a special prestige. It is known as 'standard English'. Originally, it was a regional dialect like any other but because this dialect was used by some of the most powerful and influential people from about the sixteenth century onwards, and with the widespread introduction of print, it became the standard form of *written* English throughout the country and eventually the world.

The voice of the poem makes several assertions about the link between status and the way you talk:

- The news can only be believed – 'thi trooth' – if it is read in a BBC accent; people would not listen if it was 'wonna yoo / scruff tokn' (lines 22–23).

- Ordinary people – 'scruff' – do not expect those with power or official positions to talk with a regional accent.

- Received pronunciation and standard English (accurately spelled) are the only 'correct' forms of English. (Notice that

Leonard uses phonetic spelling and does not put capital letters after his full stops.)

- Received pronunciation is also linked to education and knowledge; 'yooz doant no thi trooth yirsellz cawz yi canny talk right.'

- Ordinary people do not therefore have a voice. They are expected to be quiet: 'belt up' (line 38).

The voice in this poem is Glaswegian, but are the attitudes listed above shared by the poet? This poem plays a trick on us – as we read it we may increasingly begin to challenge what Leonard is saying, and realise he is adopting an **ironic** stance, i.e. he is pretending to express a widely held idea while actually trying to show the falseness of a set of attitudes which label so many people as inferior, simply because of their accent.

You could also consider the effect of the words on the page; how did you react when you first saw the poem? When we see English written down we expect it to be spelled in a standard way. By inventing a spelling to represent how a Glaswegian would say the words (phonetic spelling) Leonard makes the accent seem less educated. This is a trick sometimes called **'eye dialect'**. For example,

 DID YOU KNOW?

Received pronunciation is spoken by at most five per cent of the millions who speak English as their mother tongue. (Indeed, those who have learned English as a second or foreign language can sound almost too perfect!)

'Are yer goin later?' represents how many educated, R.P. speakers might *say* those words quickly, but written down it looks incorrect.

CHECK THE NET

If you look up 'Tom Leonard' you will find several sites which deal with his political attitudes and views about writing poetry.

What if the poet had written 'The reason I talk with a BBC accent is because you wouldn't want me to talk about the truth with a voice like one of you scruffy people, you wouldn't think it was true'? Would your reactions to the words be different?

The re-writing above also makes another change; the words are set out in a conventional way. Leonard's choice of poetic form chops up the words into short groups, sometimes making a line break between two words we expect to see together. This also makes the writing look odd.

Links

Political and social comment
- Nothing's Changed
- Two Scavengers...
- Vultures
- What Were They Like?
- Not My Business

Spoken voice
- Limbo
- Half-Caste

Language
- Search For My Tongue
- Half-Caste

Sense of Identity
- Limbo
- Island Man
- Search For My Tongue
- Half-Caste
- Love After Love
- Presents from My Aunts...
- Hurricane Hits England

Unusual Form
- Limbo
- What Were They Like?
- Search For My Tongue

Now take a break!

JOHN AGARD— Half-Caste

1 A 'half-caste' narrator delivers a monologue. The reader becomes the captive listener off whom the speaker bounces his thoughts.

2 The term 'half-caste' is taken literally and seems absurd.

3 As in all good satire, the true daftness lies not in the ridiculous ideas but human nature.

Part of the fun lies in the sheer energy of the speaking voice and the natural rhythms of the poet's distinctive dialect. Try reading this poem aloud!

The poet is very alert to conversational strategies and shifts of tone and attitude. The opening 'Excuse me', for instance, seems like an apology but is it truly an apology, or is the speaker adopting an attitude of mock humility, while, in fact, attacking our acceptance of the term 'half-caste'? 'Excuse me' is also a common conversational opener. (Imagine the speaker met you at a party or wanted to ask you the way in the street.).

? DID YOU KNOW?
Although its exact origin is obscure, it is believed that the term 'half-caste' was originally used of marriages between Indians and Europeans.

In any case, the bizarre proposition that because a person is somehow half *cast* (like half a plaster statue) or only half made and

CHECKPOINT 15

Apart from the joke about 'half-caste' / half cast, what other humorous play on words is introduced in the first three lines?

that therefore s/he should have only one leg to stand on, becomes the springboard for the poem's development.

With a lightly puzzled air – note the repeated use of 'wha yu mean' and 'explain yuself' – the speaker challenges us to define the term 'half-caste'. S/he speculates about possible answers and a definition of 'half-casteness' by turning the concept inside out. The logic runs: if 'half-caste' means 'a mixture', then mixtures should be called 'half-caste'.

Following this principle, the speaker offers some examples of what we might mean when we say 'half-caste':

- The famous painter, Picasso, *mixed* 'red an green', so logically he produced a 'half-caste canvas' (lines 8–9).

- The weather, particularly English weather, is a *mixture* of 'light an shadow', so logically it is 'a half-caste weather' (lines 13–15) – though s/he also adds a pun about it usually being overcast as well.

- The famous composer, Tchaikovsky, *mixed* 'a black key wid a white key' on the piano, so logically he produced 'a half-caste symphony' (lines 28–30).

Of course, such thoughts are ridiculous. In each case the result of the mixture is something *whole*, not half of anything. By the same token, 'half-castes' may be of mixed race but they are whole people.

In the next section, the speaker builds upon the opening joke about standing on one leg. Again there is a bizarre logic at work: *if the term 'half-caste' suggests s/he is, in essence, a half, then everything s/he is and does should in some way be in halves. Consequently, s/he uses half an ear, half an eye, and half a hand, dreams half a dream and casts half a shadow.* Once again these comical ideas are clearly absurd and so then is the term 'half-caste'.

Finally, the speaker turns the tables on the listener: 'but yu must come back tomorrow / wid the whole of yu eye / ...ear / ...mind' (lines 47–50). The implication is that it isn't mixed-race people who are deficient, but those who ignorantly label them as 'half-caste'. There is, as the speaker implies, more to life than appearances; there is the 'other half' (line 52) of his/her story.

Links

First person/spoken voice
- Limbo
- Nothing's Changed
- Night of the Scorpion
- Search For My Tongue
- This Room
- Not My Business
- Presents from my Aunts…
- Hurricane Hits England

Language
- Search For My Tongue
- Unrelated Incidents

Sense of Identity
- Limbo
- Island Man
- Search For My Tongue
- Unrelated Incidents
- Love After Love
- Presents from My Aunts…
- Hurricane Hits England

Repetition
- Limbo
- Night of the Scorpion
- What Were They Like?
- Not My Business

DEREK WALCOTT – Love After Love

❶ Stages of love are considered.

❷ What sort of love is deliberately left open to the reader's interpretation.

Poems may not always possess clear-cut meanings. This is such a poem. Logically, the poem seems to describe impossibilities:

❶ Full of excitement, you will experience a time when 'You will greet yourself' (line 3).

EXAMINER'S SECRET

Nobody can say exactly what 'Love After Love' means. You will gain marks if you show there is more than one possible interpretation.

2 You will sit down and eat with 'the stranger who was your self' (line 7).

3 Now you will turn to the person, yourself, whom you have ignored all your life and will enjoy life to the full.

Clearly the way into this poem is not to work with its literal sense – how can one possibly meet oneself? – but to engage one's imagination in what it suggests.

DID YOU KNOW?

Other poets in other cultures have also linked bread, wine and love; for example, in the *Rubaiyat* of Omar Khayyam: 'a jug of wine, a loaf of bread, and thou...'.

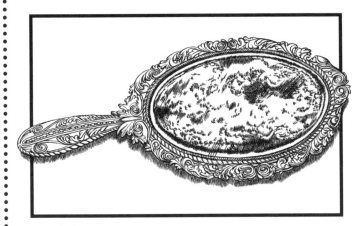

First, the tone is mainly celebratory, firmly anticipating future joy. 'Elation' (line 2), 'smile' (line 5), 'welcome' (line 5), 'love' (line 7), 'Feast' (line 15) all suggest warmth and hospitality. There is a free flow of pleasure, emphasised by the use of **enjambment** so that the sense runs on from one line to another (e.g. lines 1–6). At the same time, the flow is punctuated by commands or invitations: 'Eat' (line 6), 'Give wine. Give bread' (line 8), 'Feast on your life' (line 15). Sharing your food with a stranger under one's roof is a traditional gesture of hospitality, but the references to bread and wine also conjure up thoughts of the Christian service of Holy Communion.

The only darker moment in this celebration is the reference to tearing down the past as represented by 'Love-letters', 'photographs', 'the desperate notes' and peeling 'your own images from the mirror' (lines 12–14). The overall feeling, then, is of stripping away the past, entering a new life and being joyously re-united with a person who has for so long been a stranger.

Of course, the poet is deliberately vague about what exactly this sense of expectancy and celebration refers to. It is open to the readers to find their own significance in the words.

Certain kinds of interpretation are possible.

- HUMAN RELATIONSHIPS: What does 'Love After Love' imply? Possibly that in our lives we have to deny our true selves in order to satisfy the conditions for loving another person, and in later life we have the chance to live for ourselves.

- SELF-DISCOVERY: Throughout our working life we relentlessly pursue our career and construct a self-image based on what we feel we ought to be our 'own images from the mirror' (line 14). This poem may be suggesting that 'The time will come' (line 1) when we can be honest with ourselves and be unencumbered with ambition or concern with what others may think of us.

> **CHECKPOINT 16**
>
> What words may suggest that sub-consciously you understand your real self better than you realise?

- RELIGIOUS: We may find echoes of the parable of the 'prodigal son' or even Christian salvation. According to the Bible, humans were created in the image of God; and Christ, the Son of God, was formed in the image of humans. The 'time will come' (line 1) when we will put aside love of earthly things and will commune with our saviour whom we will recognize in ourselves. It is a complicated connection but think about the references to mirrors and images (line 14).

- AUTOBIOGRAPHICAL: We may see aspects of the poet returning to his roots. Derek Walcott grew up in a remote West Indian island but is steeped in English and European culture and teaches in an American university. Certainly much of his poetry explores the relationship between West Indian and wider cultures.

- SAD: Some may see the whole poem rather differently, not as a joyful poem but reflecting a sense of waste that it has taken so long for a person to have the confidence to value (love) him/herself, instead of anxiously seeking the approval of others.

Links

Human attitudes and relationships
- Two Scavengers…
- Night of the Scorpion
- Vultures
- What Were They Like?
- Love After Love
- Not My Business

Powerful image(s)
- Nothing's Changed
- Blessing
- Vultures

- Love After Love
- This Room

Extended metaphor
- This Room

Sense of identity
- Limbo
- Island Man
- Search For My Tongue
- Unrelated Incidents
- Half-Caste
- Presents from My Aunts…
- Hurricane Hits England

IMTIAZ DHARKER – This Room

CHECKPOINT 17

What words suggest that Dharker sees the room's walls in a negative light?

❶ The room becomes alive and breaks free in search of light and space.

❷ The furniture in the room rises up and escapes its dark confinement.

❸ The movement gathers pace and the speaker rejoices in the excitement.

❹ The speaker is left wondering what it means to be swept up in excitement.

Like 'Love After Love', this poem calls upon the reader to draw out its possible meanings. Like Walcott's poem, 'This Room' involves a sense of celebration and release. A useful starting point for looking at this poem is to consider what we may associate with rooms:

- They are where we live.

- They are private places that belong to us and where we belong.

- Rooms separate people.

- We furnish our rooms in our own personal way.

- They are confined places with walls.

- We shut out other people from our rooms.

The room as a metaphor

We may think of the room as a **metaphor** for culture. Cultures are often contained within national boundaries. Language, religion, race, social customs and behaviour can form invisible walls keeping others from understanding what happens in the 'room' (line 1). We know all too well that these barriers breed ignorance and hatred.

The furniture may be seen as representing all those private customs and beliefs that clutter our lives and create ignorance of the outside world. The poet imagines a revolution and a new beginning: 'This is the time and place / to be alive' (lines 10–11). There is a sense of movement from darkness into light; the new situation is referred to in positive terms of 'space, light' (line 4), 'celebration' (line 15) and the 'clapping' of hands (line 22). The poet celebrates the possibility of a world free from narrow prejudice as the 'room' explodes into free space. The opening description of the room 'cracking through / its own walls' (lines 3–4) perhaps reminds us of a chick breaking out of its shell to a new life.

A sense of immediacy (happening now) is created by the use of the present tense. In the first two stanzas the poet makes frequent use of participle forms: 'breaking', 'cracking', 'lifting', 'rising'. These have the effect of suggesting vigorous activity, more so than the simple verb forms, 'breaks', 'cracks', etc. The room is associated with 'nightmares' and 'dark corners' (lines 7–8).

 DID YOU KNOW?

Imtiaz Dhaker may be deliberately echoing famous lines on the French Revolution by William Wordsworth: 'Bliss was it in that dawn to be alive' (*The Prelude*, 1850)

The central stanza is rather like breathing in fresh air after escaping the musty confines of the room. The world celebrates a new order. In tune with this notion, the poet throws together a rather 'improbable' (line 13) assembly of objects and effects. There are rhymes, partial rhymes, and sound symbolism, interwoven to produce a joyous clatter: 'alive', 'lives', 'arrives'; and 'pans bang', 'clang', 'fan' (lines 11–17).

The reference to 'the daily furniture of our lives' (line 12) can also be seen as metaphorical. Household objects can be useful and necessary but also a burden (think about the stress of moving house!). Here they may represent the way in which the familiar routine events of our ordinary everyday lives can suddenly be changed. We are told not what precisely is happening, only that is it something unforeseen and unlikely – 'improbable' (line 13) – so the reader can only speculate on what is bringing about this transformation.

> **CHECKPOINT 18**
>
> What kinds of feelings are suggested in the last four lines of the poem?

Links

Extended metaphor
- Love After Love

First person point of view
- Limbo
- Nothing's Changed
- Night of the Scorpion
- Search For My Tongue
- Half-Caste
- Not My Business
- Presents from my Aunts...
- Hurricane Hits England

Contrasting cultures (and prejudice)
- Nothing's Changed
- Two Scavengers...
- Night of the Scorpion
- What Were They Like?
- Unrelated Incidents

Powerful image(s)
- Nothing's Changed
- Blessing
- Vultures
- Love After Love

Now take a break!

NIYI OSUNDARE – Not My Business

1 Akanni is beaten up and taken away in a jeep. The narrator does not see it as his business so long as he has his yam.

2 Danladi is taken away in the middle of the night. Once again, the narrator does not see it as his business so long as he has his yam.

3 Chinwe finds she has been dismissed from her job without warning. For a third time, the narrator does not see it as his business so long as he has his yam.

4 Finally, the narrator has just settled to eat his yam, when there is a knock at the door and this time it is he who is led to the waiting jeep.

This is a dark poem. Its strength lies in its simplicity but it is actually a fable, a story with a moral.

The first three stanzas each seem to be about a separate incident, which does not affect the narrator. In the fourth stanza we realise that the narrator was wrong to see what has happened to the others as '*Not My Business*' and simply be concerned about his own survival, represented in this poem by the yam – i.e. having enough to eat.

The form of the poem echoes the narrator's sense of detachment. His lack of concern is emphasised by the use of the same unthinking words each time and his reactions are separated off by the poem's layout from the description of what has happened to the others. The poet suggests that by not getting involved and appearing to accept the fate of the others, the narrator has brought about his own downfall: 'And then' (line 22). The final stanza is also only four lines long; now there is no one left to act as an unconcerned observer. It is only his lawn that reflects any human reaction by being 'bewildered' (line 25) and the silence that was the narrator's response is now the ominous silence of the waiting jeep.

If we look more closely at the way the narrator describes what happened to the others, we can pick up clues that his detachment is

 DID YOU KNOW?

There is a long history of fables and storytelling using threes; for example, three wishes, three blind mice, three wise men, Goldilocks and the three bears, etc.

CHECKPOINT 19

What important difference is there in the way the narrator identifies the victims and their enemies?

more assumed than real, to hide cowardly feelings which he is reluctant to admit to. He is very aware of what happens. We are given vivid details of how Akanni is treated brutally, as if he were made of clay, not flesh and blood, and the jeep seems to gobble him up as they 'stuffed him down' the jeep's 'belly' (line 3). Danladi also met with violence – 'booted', 'dragged' (lines 9–10) – and is abducted. Chinwe was treated very unjustly despite her 'stainless record' (line 18) and the absence of any fault – 'no' is repeated three times (line 17).

 DID YOU KNOW?

St Peter also ultimately shared Christ's fate of crucifixion.

Ironically, we do not need to be told what will happen to the narrator; the jeep mentioned in the first stanza returns for him, and he will share Akanni's fate. We are reminded of the Biblical story of St Peter denying three times that he was one of Jesus' disciples, to escape being arrested and tried.

'Not My Business' has its roots in Nigeria's civil war and military dictatorship. At the same time, the poem raises wider questions for us all. To what extent are we ready to give up comfort to defend truth and justice? Even though we may not be confronted by the secret police in the middle of the night, there may be times when we should not put our personal convenience first.

Links

Political and social comment

- Nothing's Changed
- Two Scavengers...
- Vultures
- What Were They Like?
- Unrelated Incidents

First person point of view

- Limbo
- Nothing's Changed
- Night of the Scorpion
- Search For My Tongue

- Half-Caste
- This Room
- Presents from my Aunts...
- Hurricane Hits England

Rhetorical effects (repetition, etc)

- Limbo
- Half-Caste
- Night of the Scorpion
- What Were They Like?

MONIZA ALVI – Presents from my Aunts in Pakistan

① A girl has received a gift of clothes from her aunts in Pakistan.

② The clothes were strange but beautiful and other family possessions fascinated her.

③ Her school friends were not impressed by her Pakistani clothes.

④ She tried to imagine the family home in Lahore, and the kind of life her aunts lived there.

⑤ She felt neither English or Pakistani: 'of no fixed nationality' (line 67).

> **CHECKPOINT 20**
>
> What specific references are there in the poem that have associations with life in Pakistan?

This poem has a strong autobiographical content and there are some specific personal references but the precise details are not important. The author has, in effect, created a **persona** out of her own experience. The reader is quickly drawn into wider thoughts about such concerns as nationality, identity, roots and belonging. In one sense, the voice is that of Moniza Alvi looking back at her teenaged

Presents from my Aunts ... continued

years but in a wider sense, it is the voice of all those who find themselves in a similar position.

The poem is constructed out of the thoughts of a girl, just entering her teens. Throughout the poem there are conflicting attitudes, shifts of points of view, mixed feelings, which seem to reflect her own mixed sense of identity.

The poem moves along as a series of comments, reflections, memories, rather than as any reasoned sequence or argument. For example, in a single section her thoughts move from jewellery to clothes in the wardrobe to cardigans from Marks and Spencer; the mirrors on the clothes lead to memories of her arrival in England.

The structure of the poem – free verse with varying length of lines, at times compressed almost to note form – e.g. 'Indian gold, dangling, filigree' (line 35) – reflects the girl's struggle to define and express her feelings. Most teenagers in some way or other ask themselves, 'Who am I?'. For this young girl, this question is even harder to answer.

For most teenagers, clothes are a statement of identity and belonging, and the girl's complex response to the presents reflects her own confused sense of her identity. The text in the first section is a procession of attractive colours: 'peacock-blue', 'glistening like an orange', 'gold and black', 'Candy-striped', 'apple-green' and 'silver-bordered'. But when she wears them she feels out of place – 'alien' (line 17) – and her school friend is not impressed; the clothes constricted and 'clung' (line 22); she feels 'aflame' but could not rise above her feelings of awkwardness – 'rise up out of its fire' (lines 23–24).

 DID YOU KNOW?

The phoenix was a mythical bird able to be reborn from its own ashes and rise out of the fire.

In contrast, western clothes may seem drab and dull – 'denim' and 'corduroy' (line 21) – but they are 'safe' and do not make her stand out. Although the writer does not specifically comment, it is perhaps incongruous (inappropriate or out of place) that her aunts, the senders of such glamorous presents, should want 'sensible' cardigans. The reference to the camel-skin lamp reinforces her mixed feelings; the 'cruelty' (line 29) of using the skin is **juxtaposed** with her sense of wonder at the rich colours – 'like stained glass' (line 33).

From line 44, the poem moves away from clothes. It is as if the literal mirrors, which are part of the embroidery on the clothes, act as a **metaphorical** mirror to reflect on the past or to act as a kind of window onto the world of her aunts. The journey to England was literally painful, because of her skin irritation – 'prickly heat had me screaming' (line 50). The life the aunts left behind was comfortable and protected – 'shaded', 'screened' (lines 61–62) – but, typically of this poet's complex view, she has also grown up aware of political upheaval – 'conflict … fractured land / throbbing' (lines 58–59) – and poverty – 'there were beggars' (line 65).

The poem ends ambivalently (without a clear view). Aware of her lack of positive clear identity, she is still looking back to Pakistan from her life in England, even as she seems to adopt the viewpoint of her aunts looking out onto the Shalimar Gardens.

> **CHECKPOINT 21**
>
> Suggest a reason why the poet refers to the aunts wanting 'cardigans from Marks and Spencers'.

Links

Sense of identity

- Limbo
- Island Man
- Search For My Tongue
- Unrelated Incidents
- Half-Caste
- Love After Love
- Hurricane Hits England

Contrasting cultures

- Nothing's Changed
- Island Man
- Two Scavengers …
- Night of the Scorpion

- What Were They Like?
- Search For My Tongue
- Unrelated Incidents
- Hurricane Hits England

First person point of view

- Limbo
- Nothing's Changed
- Night of the Scorpion
- Search For My Tongue
- Half-Caste
- This Room
- Not My Business
- Hurricane Hits England

GRACE NICHOLS – Hurricane Hits England

1 The noise and violence of the hurricane at night are described.

2 The poet invokes (calls on) the ancient gods of storm, thunder and wind, as if she were back in the Caribbean.

3 The poet wonders if the destruction has any meaning or purpose.

4 Suddenly she feels at one with the hurricane, as if she is part of the storm.

5 She re-establishes the bond with nature that can exist wherever you live in the world: 'the earth is the earth is the earth' (line 36).

This poem is based on Grace Nichols' experience of a real hurricane which hit the south of England in 1987; notice how the title of the poem reads like a kind of headline. However, although hurricanes are very rare in Britain, the focus of the poem in not so much on the event itself, as on the way that the violent storm re-awakens memories of her childhood in the Caribbean.

DID YOU KNOW?

The American writer, Gertrude Stein, wrote the famous and much imitated line, 'A rose is a rose is a rose is a rose is a rose' (*Sacred Emily*, 1913).

DID YOU KNOW?

The English word 'hurricane' has its origins in a Caribbean word; Hurican is the god of storms.

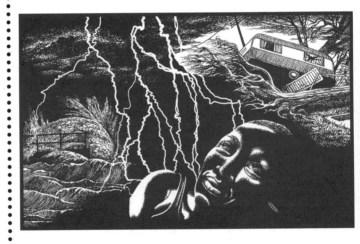

The poem begins by setting up a kind of puzzle: how can a hurricane bring someone closer to the landscape, particularly when it seems so ferocious – 'howling,', 'rage', 'dark', 'spectre' (lines 4–6)?

This puzzle is reinforced by a **paradoxical** line: the hurricane is 'Fearful and reassuring' (line 7) in the same way that illumination is 'blinding' (line 19).

The poet's struggle to think through her response to the hurricane is also reflected in her choice of point of view. Lines 1–7 are about an unknown third person 'she'. This then turns into a first person account – 'me' and 'I' – as if the poet has to confront the storm and the issues directly.

In some ways this word 'hurricane' can be seen as a symbol of the way the storm presents a fusion (blending together) of the Caribbean and the English aspects of the poet's experience. Hurricanes are alien and frightening in England but this one evokes two kinds of feelings in Grace Nichols: it is both 'reassuring', because she has experienced storms like this as a child in the Caribbean, and 'Fearful' – the feeling she shares with rest of the inhabitants of the south coast (line 7). Ultimately she finds it a liberating and defining experience.

Links

Sense of identity

- Limbo
- Island Man
- Search For My Tongue
- Unrelated Incidents
- Half-Caste
- Love After Love
- Presents from my Aunts...

First person point of view

- Limbo
- Nothing's Changed
- Night of the Scorpion
- Search For My Tongue

- Half-Caste
- This Room
- Not My Business
- Presents from my Aunts...

Sense of place

- Nothing's Changed
- Island Man
- Blessing
- Two Scavengers...
- Night of the Scorpion
- Vultures
- What Were They Like?

CHECKPOINT 22

What other paradox appears in the third stanza?

DID YOU KNOW?

We talk of ideas coming to us in a 'blinding flash'.

CHECKPOINT 23

What remarks suggest that the poet feels liberated by the storm?

From which poem?

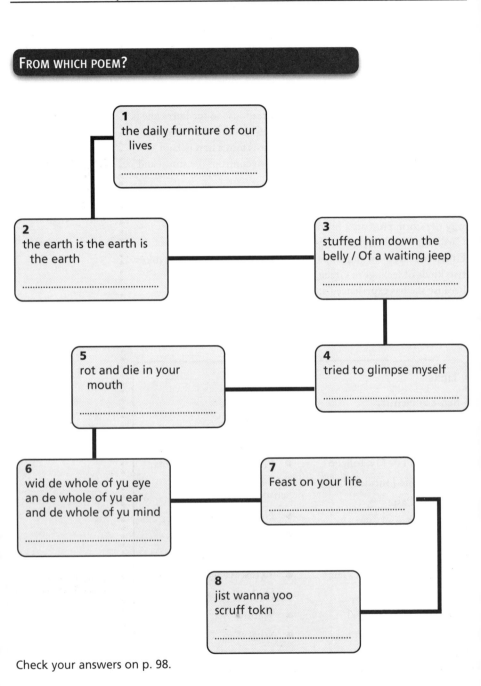

1
the daily furniture of our
   lives

....

2
the earth is the earth is
   the earth

....

3
stuffed him down the
belly / Of a waiting jeep

....

5
rot and die in your
   mouth

....

4
tried to glimpse myself

....

6
wid de whole of yu eye
an de whole of yu ear
and de whole of yu mind

....

7
Feast on your life

....

8
jist wanna yoo
scruff tokn

....

Check your answers on p. 98.

PART THREE

COMMENTARY

THEMES

This section examines some of the most common themes and ideas explored in the 'Different Cultures' section of the Anthology. The list is not exhaustive. You will see that poems appear under more than one heading because it is impossible to claim that any poem is 'about' only one subject.

It would also be possible to arrange the poems under different headings. For instance, 'Two Scavengers in a Truck ...' could easily be included in the section, 'Questions about humanity' but to do so would involve needless repetition of what has already been discussed. However, you should be aware of the possibility of using the poems for different purposes than suggested in this section.

IDENTITY

Identity and belonging

'Who am I?' may seem a strange question to ask but the answer may not be as simple as it might at first appear. Although we are all individuals with our personal likes and dislikes, our private dreams and anxieties and so on, we also have a need to belong to something larger and wider than ourselves. For example, those who support a football side want to feel part of the team and be able to boast, '*We are the champions!*'

It seems that without the reassurance of a sense of belonging, many people feel anxious and insecure. The problem is particularly acute for those who occupy a place in more than one culture.

Many young people studying the Anthology will have personal experience of this situation, which is sharply brought out in **'Presents from my Aunts in Pakistan'** by Moniza Alvi. The narrator (in effect the writer herself) has to confront the problem of being caught between two cultures. Trying on the glittering costumes sent to her from Pakistan makes her feel uncomfortable:

EXAMINER'S SECRET

You will gain marks if you can link poems to the kinds of themes and ideas outlined in this section.

**CHECK
THE NET**

Look up 'identity' or
'identity crisis' to
gain some insight
into the huge range
of issues involved.

'an alien in the sitting-room' (line 17). She longs for the safety of
English 'denim and corduroy' (line 22) but is nevertheless haunted
by images of a place from a past she can only imagine but that she
feels 'of no fixed nationality' (lines 67). The poem offers no
solutions. The narrator feels excluded from the world of her birth;
she 'could never be as lovely as those clothes' (lines 18–19) but is
unable to share her feelings with her English school-friend either.

'Love After Love' has the question of personal identity and finding
one's true self at its centre. The poet talks of greeting yourself
'arriving / At your own door' (lines 3–4) so that eventually you can
'Feast on your life' (line 15) in celebration of self-discovery. There is
no reference to any particular culture in the poem. However, the
poet Derek Walcott has had a lifelong interest in the relationship
between his native Caribbean traditions and the wider English and
European culture. Consequently, one reasonable interpretation
would be to suggest that the poem concerns being true to your
origins or perhaps enriching yourself and your culture by drawing
traditions together, rather than setting them apart.

Identity and language

Personal and social identity is closely linked with language. To an extent, both individuals and societies are shaped by the language they speak. Your native language may be the one thing that is shared with other members of your community, country or race. Even within the United Kingdom, minority languages such as Welsh and Gaelic are jealously guarded for this very reason.

Two poets, Sujata Bhatt and Tom Leonard, consider the significance of their personal language head on, as it were. In (from) '**Search For My Tongue**' the issue of continuing to use one's native language is more than a question of personal whim or nostalgia; it concerns the need to feel a whole person, which is why the poet uses images of organic growth. She suggests that her mother tongue grows spontaneously from within – 'the bud opens in my mouth' (line 34) – and its renewal is not a matter of conscious choice. Interestingly, the poet who has moved between India, the United States and Germany writes in English, which she now calls 'my language', but is a distinguished translator of Gujarati poetry into English.

Tom Leonard takes a much more aggressive attitude in (from) '**Unrelated Incidents**'. For Leonard, the use of Glaswegian English is more than an assertion of local origin. It is a political statement of identity with an oppressed and ignored section of British humanity, namely the working class. He sees the use of standard English and received pronunciation (BBC English) as a means of cultural dominance. The proof, he would claim, is that we are meant to *trust* those who speak supposedly 'properly' and disregard those who do not, and the news agenda is controlled by the well-spoken people in London.

Consequently, the poem is a kind of stand against linguistic colonialism that steals the identity of people such as working-class Glaswegians. For this reason, Leonard's poem is an active assertion of identity and demand for respect.

Language as a source of identity is also built in to several other poems in the Anthology. Edward Brathwaite in '**Limbo**', for instance, mimics the rhythmic music of the African slaves. Its

DID YOU KNOW?

IRA prisoners deliberately learned Irish Gaelic as in the past the English had tried to stamp it out.

CHECK THE NET

Look up 'Rab C. Nesbitt' the string-vested, working class Glaswegian philosopher, played by Gregor Fisher in the BBC comedy series. Do we laugh at the character or the accent?

DID YOU KNOW?

As recently as 2002, a lawyer criticised a nervous witness for speaking in a regional dialect, and not 'the Queen's English'.

DID YOU KNOW?

Many West Indian poets are 'performance poets' and read their poems to musical accompaniment. One of the best known is Linton Kwesi Johnson who even has his own record label.

extensive use of repetition, alliteration and compressed grammatical forms, e.g. 'stick is the whip / and the dark deck is slavery' (lines 20–21), is only a step away from rap music. Grace Nichols' **'Hurricane Hits England'** uses more conventional language but when the subject turns to West Indian sources, the distinctive Caribbean voice breaks through:

> Talk to me Huracan
> Talk to me Oya
> Talk to me Shango
> And Hattie,
> My sweeping, back-home cousin'

(lines 8–12)

John Agard's **'Half-Caste'** is, of course, all about personal identity but his use of a Caribbean voice establishes an identity as forcible as his witty argument, particularly as the dialect seems to force out the more conventional standard English forms:

> I close half-a-eye
> consequently when I dream
> I dream half-a-dream
> *An when moon begin to glow*
> *I half-caste human being ...*

(lines 41–45)

(See also **Language and style**.)

ROOTS

Closely associated with the question of identity is the notion of roots. In some ways 'roots' is a curious word to use in connection with human beings because we associate roots with plants and being fixed and immobile. Think of the expression 'rooted to the spot'. Human beings, on the other hand, are free to move wherever they want and to travel is a major ambition for many people. Nevertheless, the urge to 'put down roots' or 'return to one's roots' is a very powerful feeling. It is partly to do with a sense of belonging and partly to do with feeling in touch with your past.

Most, if not all, of the poets represented in the Anthology are in a sense displaced persons and have moved away from their 'roots', if only because of their education and lifestyle as international poets and scholars. Perhaps it is because of this separation that so many of them are compelled to express a connection with their origins.

Most obviously, we define our roots as the place in which we were born and bred. Grace Nichols makes clear the way in which you can be haunted by your feelings for the country from which you came. **'Island Man'** demonstrates that the link with one's birthplace can never truly be severed. The mind of the man in question inhabits the Caribbean and hears the 'sound of blue surf' (line 3) even if his body wakes up to the 'surge of wheels' on the 'dull North Circular' (lines 14–15).

'Hurricane Hits England' adds a slightly different perspective. The freak storm that spread so much terror through southern England proves strangely comforting to the poet. She no longer feels an alien in England, cut off from her roots. The hurricane, a familiar phenomenon in the Caribbean, bridges the gap so that she can feel that 'the earth is the earth is the earth' (line 36) and that her roots have spread to her new home.

DID YOU KNOW?

The American author Alex Hayley traced his own roots back to a village in the Gambia and his quest was dramatised in a famous TV series called *Roots*, first shown in 1975.

DID YOU KNOW?

Hurricanes were traditionally given female names by weather forecasters. In the interest of equality, male and female names now alternate.

Roots need not relate to a physical place. We have already seen in (from) **'Search For My Tongue'** how Sujata Bhatt searches for her identity in the use of her mother tongue. It could equally be said that the language Gujarati represents her roots, especially as her feel for the language is expressed in plant imagery.

Kamau Brathwaite's **'Limbo'** draws on emotional roots and a living awareness of African history rather than personal memory. There is a sense of a shared tradition that has passed down through black music and song. What is more, the poet uses a collective African tradition with its pulsating rhythms to breathe life and originality into the English literary tradition.

CULTURAL DIFFERENCES

The question of identity and roots largely arises from the fact that individuals and societies are faced with differences and conflicts between cultures; people who live a settled life within a single culture have no need to question where they belong or concern themselves with other cultures. Some poems deal with cultural difference very directly at a personal level.

We have seen how the young girl in **'Presents from my Aunts in Pakistan'** is acutely aware of the clash between her familiar English teenage culture and her family's distant background in Pakistan. Similarly, (from) **'Search For My Tongue'** represents a personal battle between two cultures as represented by English and Gujarati.

Grace Nichols' **'Island Man'** and **'Hurricane Hits England'** both consider how our physical environment affects us and how the place in which we grow up is forever embedded in our consciousness.

In **'Night of the Scorpion'** cultural difference is less obvious because the events take place within a single community. However, there is a clear distinction between the traditional attitudes of the peasant neighbours and the detachment of the narrator who seems entirely sceptical, despite being the suffering woman's son. The narrator, who belongs to a modern educated class and is looking back on the events, seems as remote as us from the rural culture he observes so coolly.

EXAMINER'S SECRET
You will gain marks if you can link and cross-reference poems.

In '**This Room**', Imtiaz Dharker seems to suggest that cultures and traditions are restrictive, and imagines people breaking out of their narrow and separate existence, as symbolised by the room. This poem offers an alternative viewpoint to those people who insist on the importance of their particular culture to the exclusion of all others.

The poet suggests there is a darker side to cultural difference. She probably has in mind the bigotry and hatred that so often accompanies political or religious fanaticism.

THE POLITICAL DIMENSION AND INJUSTICE

Sadly, cultural differences breed suspicion and distrust, which are often born out of ignorance. Denise Levertov's '**What Were They Like?**' is a disturbing poem because it questions the brutal simplifications that arise when one civilisation is at war with another. The poet bitterly attacks the ways in which, during the Vietnam War, American propaganda effectively denied the Vietnamese people having any kind of cultural identity. They were simply 'the enemy'. She also implies that American society, and by extension Western society, is incapable of recognising or appreciating any way of life except its own.

DID YOU KNOW?
During the First and Second World Wars, the Germans were commonly referred to simply as 'Bosch' or 'The Hun'.

Perhaps the sharpest cultural divide is not to do with customs or traditions but lies between rich and poor. Lawrence Ferlinghetti

CHECK THE NET

'American dream' is one of the most powerful and persuasive phrases in the modern world. If you look it up, you will find about two million sites!

exposes this gulf very cleverly in **'Two Scavengers in a Truck, Two Beautiful People in a Mercedes'**. By physically drawing the two ends of society together through the chance meeting at the traffic lights, he is able to highlight the huge inequalities that exist within a society that prides itself in offering opportunities for all. There are numerous **ironic** parallels and contrasts explored throughout the poem but it is perhaps the image of the sunglasses that seems to capture the essence of the divide between the two couples. For the architect in his linen suit, they are a fashion accessory, part of the total 'ensemble'. For the garbageman they seem to represent a hopeless attempt to ape the 'cool' lifestyle of the rich.

The divide between rich and poor also lies at the heart of **'Nothing's Changed'**. The legacy of apartheid still casts its shadow – 'whites only inn' (line 24) – but it is not the question of colour that dominates the poem. Like Ferlinghetti, Tatamkhulu Afrika sets images of wealth and poverty side by side. The poet seethes with anger that such conspicuous, cultivated consumption symbolised by the 'single rose' (line 32) on the linen tablecloth can exist in the midst of widespread poverty, represented by the 'plastic table's top' (line 37).

'Limbo' offers another picture of oppression and injustice. Edward Kamau Brathwaite is inspired to recreate in words the vibrant qualities of the slaves' music. Nevertheless, he paints a frightening picture of the life of people who have been stripped of all dignity. Music is their only salvation – 'the music is saving me' (line 47).

Even such a joyous poem as Imtiaz Dharker's **'Blessing'** draws our attention to the plight of the most deprived in society. The image of the children 'screaming in the liquid sun' (line 19) catches people's natural zest for life. At the same time, the final reference to the children's 'small bones' (line 23) connects with the opening words, 'The skin cracks like a pod' (line 1). In this way we are reminded that the burst main is only the briefest relief from unremitting poverty. Although there is no direct contrast with the rich in this poem, we clearly understand where the municipal pipe normally leads.

SENSE OF PLACE

None of the poems is concerned with describing places for their own sake. However, a sense of place plays an important role in several poems.

In fact, Tatamkhula Afrika's identification with District Six in **'Nothing's Changed'** is crucial to his response to what he sees there. For the reader, it is a rather inhospitable, run down, stony area, strewn with discarded cans and overgrown with weeds. However, we are asked to understand that this unremarkable wasteland is an extension of the writer himself. It represents a personal history of the struggle to free South Africa from the oppression of the apartheid era and continues to symbolise Afrika's own anger at the continuing gulf between rich and poor. It is more than a mere place; it is, in effect, a physical embodiment of passionate emotion.

Lawrence Ferlinghetti sets **'Two Scavengers in a Truck, Two Beautiful People in a Mercedes'** specifically in 'downtown San Francisco' (line 2). In one sense, the situation the poem describes could take place in any modern city. However, by choosing San Francisco, Ferlinghetti is able to draw on familiar images of the Californian sun and the 'American dream'. In fact, the precise setting is not described beyond the mention of the traffic light but readers from all round the world can easily provide the backdrop, as in a sense, we have all visited San Francisco at our local cinema.

A similar play upon familiar images is found in Grace Nichols' **'Island Man'**. The West Indian, waking to the roar of London's traffic, dreams of home. However, his dreams consist of familiar images of an island 'paradise'. The very phrase 'small emerald island' (line 10) is virtually a **cliché**. His memories do not appear to include poverty and hopelessness, so we have to presume he came to England in order to escape. The point is, of course, that nostalgia is a kind of forgetfulness. We remember only the best of what we have left behind.

Chinua Achebe's **'Vultures'** is not about a place at all but the image of the brooding vultures perched on a bare branch in the African

CHECKPOINT 24
Why do you think the event takes place in a 'downtown' area?

bush lends the poem a distinctive power. The physical image of the 'despondent dawn' and the 'broken bone of a dead tree' (lines 2–6) lays the ground for the poem's concern with the darker side of human nature.

'**Limbo**' is set on board a ship transporting African slaves. The ship is not described but there are frequent and repetitive references to the deck and the surrounding darkness. The result is a claustrophobic (shut in) effect. The slaves' whole lives are bounded by the deck and the darkness. There is no relief from this physical and mental prison except through their music.

QUESTIONS ABOUT HUMANITY

Two poems, '**Vultures**' by Chinua Achebe and '**Not My Business**' by Niyi Osundare, consider the darker side of human nature. Both are Nigerian, and write against the history of a savage civil war and many years of military dictatorship that came to an end as recently as 1999. However, both poets draw on their experience to question aspects of humanity as a whole.

 DID YOU KNOW?

Bergen-Belsen's most infamous commandant was SS officer, Josef Kramer. It was never an extermination camp but under his regime, 18,000 prisoners died of starvation and typhoid in a single month.

Achebe introduces the disturbing thought that good and evil are inseparable, that one cannot exist without the other. The

Commandant at Belsen may seem an exceptional case but is his cruelty to his prisoners mixed with his love for his daughter not part of the natural order of things, just like the vultures?

Osundare reflects upon complacency and cowardice in the face of evil and injustice. How far are we prepared to speak out and stand up for what is right? So long as we are comfortable, do we care?

Apart from being a specific attack on American policy during the Vietnam War, **'What Were They Like?'** also raises questions about wider human attitudes. To what extent are we indifferent to the suffering of those who do not touch our personal lives in any way?

PEOPLE

There are very few people referred to directly in the poems. Even when people are described, as in **'Two Scavengers...'**, we are invited to consider what their appearance represents and what it tells us about society. In **'Not My Business'** the poet uses the people named as representatives of the oppressed, rather than as individuals. Again, in **'Night of the Scorpion'** the neighbours are presented as the voice of superstition and prejudice rather than as a group of individuals.

However, many of the poems represent the voice of an individual, such as **'Nothing's Changed'**, which is clearly based on the poet's personal experience. But it is often better to think of the poet as adopting the role of a **persona**. For example, the teenage girl at the centre of **'Presents from my Aunts...'** may well be based on the experiences of a young Moniza Alvi, but you should think of the girl as a character who can stand for anyone in a similar situation.

Sometimes poets identify with characters that are not based on direct personal experience. For instance in **'Limbo'**, Brathwaite projects himself into the mind of a nineteenth-century slave. Even though Nichols shares her West Indian origins with the imaginary **'Island Man'**, her particular background and experience would be very different.

In short, poets are more concerned with capturing human experience that we can all share, than describing the outward features of individuals.

DID YOU KNOW?

There is a term, 'nimby' (not in my back yard), that is used of people who do not want their own comfortable life disturbed.

People who are referred to directly or discussed

- Two Scavengers in a Truck …
  The couple in the Mercedes and the garbagemen

- Nothing's Changed
  The diners at the 'up-market, haute cuisine' (line 22) restaurant. Their lifestyle is suggested through the details of the restaurant and may resemble that of the couple in the Mercedes
  The working men in the café, again described through details of the food, the table top, etc.

- Blessing
  The inhabitants of the shanty town whose lack of water causes their skin to crack 'like a pod' (line 1).
  The joyful children

- Limbo
  The African slaves being transported on board ship

- Not my Business
  Akanni, Danladi, Chinwe, acquaintances of the narrator, who are taken away by the security service

- What Were They Like?
  The people of Vietnam and their customs

- Island Man
  A West Indian nostalgic for his homeland

- Night of the Scorpion
  The peasant neighbours and their superstitions
  The 'rationalist' (line 36) father
  The holy man and his 'rites' (line 42)
  The suffering mother

- Vultures
  The Commandant of Belsen

- Presents from my Aunts in Pakistan
  Aunt Jamila who is at ease with Pakistani culture
  The school-friend who is not impressed by her presents
  The Aunts themselves 'in shaded rooms, screened from male visitors' (lines 61–62)

EXAMINER'S SECRET
Remember to consider why these people are included. Are they presented as individuals or representative of a group?

People behind the voice of the narrator

- Nothing's Changed
  An African who has fought for freedom from white oppression discovering that the divide between the rich white people and the poor black people is as wide as ever

- Night of the Scorpion
  A child who looks on at the events in the hut like a detached observer

- (From) Search For My Tongue
  An Indian living in an English-speaking country who struggles to recover her identity through her mother tongue, Gujarati

- Unrelated Incidents
  A working class Glaswegian who resents the dominance of standard English and received pronunciation

- Half-Caste
  A person of mixed race who challenges our assumptions about his colour

- Not My Business
  A person who sees his friends being beaten up and taken away by the security services but does nothing because he has his yam to savour

- Presents from my Aunts in Pakistan
  A thirteen-year-old girl born in Pakistan but brought up in England, who feels trapped between two competing cultures

- Hurricane Hits England
  A West Indian living in England who feels the great storm of 1987 has put her in touch with her roots once again

EXAMINER'S SECRET
Make lists like this for different themes to help you with your revision.

 Now take a break!

LANGUAGE AND STYLE

POETRY AND SPEECH

EXAMINER'S SECRET

Any sensible comments on language and style will improve your grade.

One fairly common feature of modern poetry is the trend to make greater use of the resources of natural speech.

English poet Tennyson's verse was quite fluid, it sounds rather grand and imposing. It's fun to say aloud but it hardly sounds like natural English:

> Below the thunders of the upper deep;
> Far, far beneath in the abysmal sea,
> His ancient, dreamless, uninvaded sleep
> The Kraken sleepeth …
>
> Alfred Tennyson: *The Kraken*, 1830

Compare that to the opening of one of the more formal poems in the Anthology, **'Vultures'**:

> In the greyness
> and the drizzle of one despondent
> dawn unstirred by harbingers
> of sunbreak a vulture
> perching high on broken
> bone of a dead tree …
>
> (lines 1–6)

The language is still very measured but it has more of the feel of natural spoken English. Why is there a difference? Tennyson uses lines of fixed, ten-syllable length within which there is a more or less regular series of five stressed syllables. Achebe, on the other hand, uses the natural stress patterns of normal speech, which are in fact pretty regular, and organises them into line units. The lines vary in length (4, 9, 7, 6, 6 and 5 syllables) but each carry equal weight, as it were, with two main stresses in each line.

The use of natural stress patterns can be traced throughout the Anthology. However, as in all poetry, the effects are extremely varied. For instance, **'Love After Love'** is warm and expansive, whilst **'Two Scavengers …'** seems dry and precise.

However, although the poets use natural stress patterns, they do not simply write as they talk. Just as poets have always done, the poets represented in the Anthology use words in special and surprising ways and use all sorts of techniques that are hardly possible in ordinary speech. For example, just like Tennyson, Achebe chooses and organises his vocabulary very precisely to produce a calculated effect (see **Detailed summaries**). Both are creating a rather mysterious, even frightening image and both poems have a sombre feel.

ORAL POETRY

If most of the poems in the Anthology borrow something from the features of natural speech, three poems, **'Half-Caste'**, (from) **'Unrelated Incidents'** and **'Limbo'**, deliberately feature a speaking voice.

'Half-Caste' is written phonetically in order to capture the sound and mannerisms of Caribbean speech ('Explain yuself wha yu mean' rather than 'Explain yourself. What do you mean?'). The poem cries out to be performed and it is impossible to appreciate its wit without 'hearing' the speaker. The same may be said of the Glaswegian voice of **'Unrelated Incidents'**.

It would be wrong, however, to suppose that these poems are somehow more spontaneous than any others. They may sound like natural speech but are very carefully crafted. For instance, look at the puns and repetitions in 'Half-Caste' or consider the way Leonard uses his phonetic spelling to make his point (see **Detailed summaries**).

'Limbo' is rather different. We are conscious of the 'sound' of a voice, but Brathwaite is not so much imitating day-to-day speech, like Agard or Leonard, as drawing on an **oral tradition**. What we hear is not strictly speech but song. The pared-down grammar using only essential words ('stick is the whip' etc.), the use of a repeated **refrain** ('limbo / limbo like me'), the repeated word patterns and the

 DID YOU KNOW?

Some of the world's oldest poems were passed down through an oral tradition before they were written down. Some of the most famous are the *Iliad* and *Odyssey* from Greece, the *Mahabharata* and *Ramayana* from India, the Old English *Beowulf* and the *Nibelung Saga* from Germany. Some African poems have only recently been recorded.

CHECK THE NET
One of the most famous songs in the Caribbean oral tradition is 'Linstead Market'. See if you can find the lyrics on the Internet.

sparse use of circumstantial detail (no descriptions of ship, slaves, weather, destination, etc.) produce something of the timeless effect that is found in folk songs. Although the poem appears to be a first person account ('like me'), it is in effect the voice of a whole people.

VARIETIES OF ENGLISH

It could be said that all poetry is written in non-standard English, in the sense that poets use words in unusual and surprising ways that you would not expect to find in a history book or newspaper report, for example. Admittedly, most poets (including most represented in the Anthology) use grammar and vocabulary drawn from standard English. However, it is also true that poets have always exploited the widest resources that language can offer, including dialect forms.

We have seen how the use of a particular form of English can express a sense of identity (see **Identity and language**). In 'Half-Caste', however, John Agard does rather more than that. He uses West Indian forms not only to establish a 'voice' but also to project a particular way of treating life.

It is dangerous to generalise, but Caribbean English is capable of a distinctive economy and directness of expression, welded to a mischievous, satirical point of view. You must be careful, however, not to exaggerate the non-standard elements in '**Half-Caste**'. In fact, John Agard cleverly adjusts standard English only very slightly. Most of the Caribbean flavour is conveyed by **non-standard spelling** or **eye dialect** with very gentle departures from standard English grammar such as 'Ah listening to yu wid de keen half of mih ear' (lines 33–34) instead of 'I am listening to you with the keen half of my ear'. Nevertheless, these minor differences are sufficient to suggest a particular way of speaking that perfectly conveys a sense of mock bewilderment at the absurdities of human behaviour.

'LINE GRAMMAR'

An important feature of poetry is that, unlike ordinary prose, it is consciously constructed as a sequence of lines. Look at this famous sentence:

I wandered lonely as a cloud that floats on high o'er vales and hills, when all at once I saw a crowd, a host, of golden daffodils; beside the lake, beneath the trees, fluttering and dancing in the breeze.

Of course, it is more familiar as the opening six lines of Wordsworth's poem of 1807, 'I Wandered Lonely As a Cloud':

> I wandered lonely as a cloud
> That floats on high o'er vales and hills,
> When all at once I saw a crowd,
> A host, of golden daffodils;
> Beside the lake, beneath the trees,
> Fluttering and dancing in the breeze.

Notice how each line is a complete unit in itself (8 syllables, 4 stresses) but that the line breaks match the natural pauses in the grammatical sense. These divisions are also reinforced by the punctuation.

Several poets represented in the Anthology, however, use line divisions in a very different way. Look at the opening sentence of **'Presents from my Aunts in Pakistan'**, for instance:

They sent me a salwar kameez peacock-blue, and another glistening like an orange split open, embossed slippers, gold and black points curling.

Written that way it is simply a list of items of clothing. Moniza Alvi, however, arranges the list so as to create a sharper focus:

> They sent me a salwar kameez
>   peacock-blue,
>   and another
>   glistening like an orange split open,
>   embossed slippers, gold and black
>   points curling.

EXAMINER'S SECRET
When dealing with language and style you will gain only very few marks for simply spotting a metaphor or an example of enjambment etc. You will gain many more marks if you can show an appreciation of their effects.

'Line grammar' continued

EXAMINER'S SECRET

Remember that in poetry words take on more than plain dictionary meanings. Think about the associations of the words too.

This time the dead list has become almost an activity, as our eye is drawn to one feature, then another. The irregular layout can also be said to be a kind of punctuation, tracing an active response to the presents. Throughout the poem, Alvi uses this 'line grammar' to reflect the sudden shifts in the girl's thought and its varying intensity. Sometimes, she will use the line to break a phrase so as to throw the emphasis on a single word, so when she says, 'I longed / for denim and corduroy' (lines 20–21) the word 'longed' is emphasised as it comes at the end of the line. In more relaxed moments, she will use more conventional line divisions with no distortion of the natural grammatical structure: 'My mother cherished her jewellery – / Indian gold, dangling, filigree' (lines 34–35).

Grace Nichols' **'Island Man'** relies very heavily indeed on 'line grammar'. The poem has no formal punctuation and the poet has deliberately provided a slightly uncertain and open-ended sentence structure. The 'line grammar', however, allows us to pick our way through the island man's drowsy consciousness. Notice, for instance, how the line divisions allow us to combine the ideas in different ways, as in a dream: '… the sound of blue surf / in his head' (lines 3–4) or 'in his head / the steady breaking and wombing' (lines 4–5).

'Two Scavengers in a Truck, Two Beautiful People in a Mercedes' uses lines to present a series of snapshots and observations, all contributing to a kind of verbal collage. Each line contains a key word or phrase ('stoplight … downtown San Francisco … garbage truck … garbagemen … standing … hanging on … looking down … Mercedes … elegant … man … hip, linen … sunglasses … blond … short skirt … architect's office …scavengers', and so on) and as we move through the poem we build up a picture of meaning. Here, again, the layout forms a kind of punctuation.

'Nothing's Changed' and **'Blessing'** also make interesting use of 'line grammar' to throw the focus on particular details but many poems, like **'Night of the Scorpion'** make use of more traditional enjambment:

> Ten hours
> of steady rain had driven him
> to crawl beneath a sack of rice.
>
> (lines 2–4)

'**Vultures**' is remarkable in that it is a case of almost continuous enjambment and the sense is a continuous flow; most lines make little sense on their own, e.g. 'mate his smooth' (line 8). On the other hand, the fact that almost no line seems complete and we have to keep reading to find a resting place gives the poem a particular drive and intensity; we cannot relax. How different from Wordsworth's lines!

EXAMINER'S SECRET

The technical aspects of poetry can be very confusing. Do not despair. Examiners are more interested in whether you have a personal feel for how a poem is written than lists of technical vocabulary.

Now take a break!

PART FOUR

RESOURCES

HOW TO USE QUOTATIONS

One of the secrets of success in writing essays is the way you use quotations. There are five basic principles:

1 Put inverted commas at the beginning and end of the quotation.

2 Write the quotation exactly as it appears in the original.

3 Do not use a quotation that repeats what you have just written.

4 Use the quotation so that it fits into your sentence.

5 Keep the quotation as short as possible.

Quotations should be used to develop the line of thought in your essays. Your comment should not duplicate what is in your quotation. For example:

> The speaker thinks that your mother tongue would die if you had to speak a foreign language, if you lived in a place you had to
> > 'speak a foreign tongue,
> > your mother tongue would rot'

Far more effective is to write:

> The speaker thinks that if you have to speak a foreign language there could be problems because she says, 'your mother tongue would rot'.

However, the most sophisticated way of using the writer's words is to embed them into your sentence:

> The poet thinks 'your mother tongue would rot' if you were required to speak a foreign language.

EXAMINER'S SECRET

You need to test yourself in some way to make sure you really do know your way around the poems. You are not required to learn the poems by heart, but if you can quote freely without looking at the text, you can feel you are getting to know the poems really well.

When you use quotations in this way, you are demonstrating the ability to use text as evidence to support your ideas – not simply including words from the original to prove you have read it.

SITTING THE EXAMINATION

Examination papers are carefully designed to give you the opportunity to do your best. Follow these handy hints for exam success:

BEFORE YOU START

- Make sure you know the subject of the examination so that you are properly prepared and equipped.

- You need to be comfortable and free from distractions. Inform the invigilator if anything is off-putting, e.g. a shaky desk.

- Read the instructions, or rubric, on the front of the examination paper. You should know by now what you have to do but check to reassure yourself.

- Observe the time allocation – and follow it carefully. If they recommend 60 minutes for Question 1 and 30 minutes for Question 2, it is because Question 1 carries twice as many marks.

- Consider the mark allocation. You should write a longer response for 4 marks than for 2 marks.

WRITING YOUR RESPONSES

- Use the questions to structure your response, e.g. question: 'The endings of X's poems are always particularly significant. Explain their importance with reference to two poems.' The first part of your answer will describe the ending of the first poem; the second part will look at the ending of the second poem; the third part will be an explanation of the significance of the two endings.

- Write a brief draft outline of your response.

EXAMINER'S SECRET

The danger is that often candidates want to write *whatever* they know about a poem regardless of whether it is relevant or not. Ask any examiner what lets down candidates the most and the answer will be *failure to answer the question*.

- A typical 30-minute examination essay is probably between 400 and 600 words in length.

- Keep your writing legible and easy to read, using paragraphs to show the structure of your answers.

- Spend a couple of minutes afterwards quickly checking for obvious errors.

WHEN YOU HAVE FINISHED

- Don't be downhearted – if you found the examination difficult, it is probably because you really worked at the questions. Let's face it, they are not meant to be easy!

- Don't pay too much attention to what your friends have to say about the paper. Everyone's experience is different and no two people ever give the same answers.

IMPROVE YOUR GRADE

KNOW YOUR TEXTS

EXAMINER'S SECRET
DO NOT rely on the fact you can take the Anthology into the examination. By then it is too late to start reading the poems.

It is vital that you know your texts. These Notes are intended to help you come to grips with the poems in the Anthology but they are no substitute for reading the poems closely yourself. Remember to say the poems aloud and get a feel for how they sound.

There are three essential aspects of the poems that you need to master:

❶ CONTENT You need to know what the words mean and understand the basic subject matter, the 'story', as it were.

❷ INTERPRETATION You need to understand what message the poet is trying to convey. Is the poet saying something about identity or injustice, for example?

❸ METHODS As well as *what* the authors have to say, you need to understand *how* they get their ideas across, especially how they use language. This is the hardest aspect of poetry to grasp but an understanding of a poet's methods can gain you the most marks.

You need to know the basic content of the poems before you can answer any question but there are only a limited number of marks available for simply giving an account of the content, however detailed.

You will have notes from your teacher and you may also use guides such as this or material gathered from the Internet. However, no matter how good this information may be, it is of little use to you unless you understand it.

You are not expected to come up with all the ideas about the poems yourself but you must make the ideas your own and work out ways of expressing ideas in your own language. You need to do this in the way that suits you best. You could for instance, work with pairs of poems, say 'Love After Love' and 'This Room' and find as many similarities and differences as you can, by thinking about ideas, the mood of the poems, vocabulary, how the authors suggest their ideas without saying exactly what they mean, etc. The answers to these questions may be scattered through the notes you have been given or you have found. It is your job to bring them together in your own way.

One way of organising your notes and ideas is to keep a quotation book. You may wonder why you need to write out quotations, when you have the poems in front of you. The point is that if you select key quotations, they sharpen your attention and help you to focus on particular points rather than looking vaguely at the poem.

Quotations are of no use unless you know what to use them for. A good idea is to list your key quotations and list the points they can illustrate alongside/beneath. For example:

Nothing's Changed
'Small round hard stones click'

- Unwelcoming environment – compare Vultures (use of setting)
- Monosyllables establish beat (rhythm) – compare Limbo (use of sound)

Notice that a single, brief quotation may serve more than one

EXAMINER'S SECRET
Examiners can easily tell if you are repeating word for word what you have read and may not be able to give you the marks you expect because you have not shown real understanding.

EXAMINER'S SECRET
There is no single or completely 'correct' interpretation of a poem and the examiners will reward a whole range of different views but they must make sense.

purpose. You can also use your quotation book to build up cross-references to other poems. There is no need to put all these points in at once; you can add them as you learn more about the poems.

Remember a quotation book works both ways. You can list what each quotation can be used for and you can find what quotations can illustrate particular points. You can also use the book to collect useful words and phrases.

EXAMINER'S SECRET

The examiners have read the poems and do not want to read long quotations or summaries of what they already know. They *do* want to know what you *think* about the texts.

Of course, it takes time to construct a quotation book but it is more useful than trying to make sense of bundles of notes at the last minute.

There are not very many marks to be gained by giving a long and detailed account of a poem. Remember for the most part poets do not simply tell stories; certainly none of the poems in the Anthology are purely narrative poems. Even where there is some sort of narrative, there is also some sort of point behind the story.

For example, '**Two Scavengers …**' recounts an incident in a San Francisco street but the poem is really about inequality, the 'American dream', rich and poor, and so on. There is not even any need to say what happens. The examiner wants you to write about the significance of what happens. To simply state that the truck and the Mercedes stop at the traffic light indicates to the examiner only that you have read the poem. If you point out that the two couples from the extremes of society are thrown together by chance, you are indicating that you understand the significance of the stop at the traffic light.

EXAMINER'S SECRET

You can *refer* to what happens in order to *make a point* but do not describe what happens.

SELECTING THE POEMS

However good your understanding of the Anthology, how well you progress in the examination depends to a large extent on careful selection of the most suitable poems to answer the question. There is little point in attempting to use 'Vultures' to write about rich and poor!

Usually, the question will name one specific poem to write about and ask you to compare it with another of your own choice. That choice is crucial.

Consider the following task:

Compare the ways in which poets present people in 'Two Scavengers in a Truck, Two Beautiful People in a Mercedes' and *one* other poem.

First, you need to decide which poems provide the best focus on people. There are some poems that make direct reference to people but you need to ask yourself if there is enough to write about. For example, there is some description of children in **'Blessing'** and a reference to the Belsen Commandant in **'Vultures'**, but how much can you really say that is relevant to the question? You could perhaps write about injustice or good and evil but it requires a great deal of skill to keep the focus on the presentation of people.

You need to decide on a poem which offers the best points of comparison or contrast. **'What Were They Like'** seems very different from **'Two Scavengers in a Truck'** but there are some clear lines you could pursue:

● Both poets have a social conscience

● The rich know little of the poor / Americans knew little of the Vietnamese

● The poor are victims

● Both poems criticise American / western society

● Both poets feel passionately about justice for people

● Ferlinghetti contrasts two extremes within society / Levertov contrasts two societies

● Ferlinghetti presents people through images of their possessions / Levertov presents people through images of their culture

● Ferlinghetti focuses on two representative couples / Levertov considers a whole nation

You need not think only of those poems in which people are referred to directly. Some of the poems present people through their

EXAMINER'S SECRET

You need to know the *kinds* of things you can say about the texts *before* you enter the examination room. If you are well prepared all you should need to do in the examination is *adapt* your ideas to the *needs of the question*.

EXAMINER'S SECRET

Examiners will do their best to reward any sensible comment but if you have chosen an unsuitable poem for the question, you are unlikely to gain the highest marks.

EXAMINER'S SECRET

The best answers are usually by candidates who have already thought about various possible combinations of poems to suit various purposes.

EXAMINER'S SECRET

Do not write about a poem simply because it's the one you know most about. Choose a poem that fits the task.

thoughts. **'Nothing's Changed'** could be a good choice. Like 'Two Scavengers in a Truck …', it explores injustice and the contrast between rich and poor. Both use material objects to highlight differences (sunglasses, the rose, the plastic table top) but whereas Ferlinghetti presents people from the outside, Afrika's poem is rooted in a man's inner thoughts.

CONSTRUCTING YOUR RESPONSE

Let's consider the question again:

> Compare the ways in which poets present people in 'Two Scavengers in a Truck, Two Beautiful People in a Mercedes' and *one* other poem.

The question does not ask you to write all you know about two poems. It directs you to think along very specific lines. Look at the key elements:

- **Compare** (not describe, outline or discuss)

- The **ways** in which poets **present** (not just what the poets tell you but how they do it)

- **People** (not place, culture, atmosphere, etc.)

- **Two texts**, one specified

You need to take account of all these factors.

Start positively

Do not waste time copying out the question or explaining what you are about to write about. Make a point in your first sentence. Rather than beginning vaguely with something on the lines of 'Ferlinghetti presents people in interesting ways and I am going to compare Ferlinghetti's poem to "Nothing's Changed"' try **'Ferlinghetti and Tatamkhulu Afrika both contrast the lifestyles of rich and poor.'**

Stick to the subject

Try to keep the question in mind as you write.

It is very easy to get carried away so that you drift off the point. For example, if you were writing about 'Two Scavengers in a Truck ...', the references to sunglasses are very important but there is no need to provide a lengthy account of the importance of sunglasses in today's fashion.

Balance your answer

It is important to keep your answer in proportion. You need to write about two poems and include a *range* of comment on both. Do not get bogged down in one narrow area of the text. If half way through your answer, you are still writing about the opening stanza of 'Two Scavengers in a Truck ...', it is unlikely you are going to say very much that is worthwhile about the rest.

WHAT THE EXAMINERS ARE LOOKING FOR

Examiners are looking for knowledge and understanding of the texts. They look for the ability to make comment and support it by reference to the text. In the words of the examination specification candidates need to 'analyse and evaluate'. In practice, the examiners recognise different *levels of response*, nine in all, ranging from unclassified to A*.

Let's consider possible treatment of the question we have already touched on:

> **Compare the ways in which poets present people in 'Two Scavengers in a Truck, Two Beautiful People in a Mercedes' and *one* other poem.**

BASIC (approximately G to E, dependent on the amount of detail) We have seen that the key words are 'compare' and 'present' but the weakest candidates will concentrate on **literal** information and probably use fairly simple vocabulary in their account. They may write along these lines:

> **In 'Two Scavengers' the two garbage men meet a man and a woman in Mercedes at traffic light. The garbage men are wearing plastic but the man and the girl are very fashionable.**

EXAMINER'S SECRET
Watch the clock! Do not save up your best point to last. You may never reach it.

You can tell this when the poet says 'with shoulder length hair & sunglasses'. The young man on the truck also wears sunglasses.

Ferlinghetti thinks it is wrong that some people should be so rich. In 'Night of the Scorpion' the neighbours all rush to see the woman who has been bitten. They say things like 'May the poison purify your flesh'. At the end the mother recovers.

- This is a very simple approach.

- There are *statements* that indicate some knowledge of the texts.

- People are *identified* and there is some related *quotation*.

- There is some simple *comment* on the couple being fashionable and the candidate sees a link with the garbageman through the reference to the sunglasses. However, the significance of the link is not explained.

- There is a *general comment* about Ferlinghetti's attitude to the rich but no explanation or illustration.

- There is no comment on how people are presented.

- The candidate is unable to do more than identify some simple *surface features* of 'Night of the Scorpion'. It may not have been the best choice of a second poem.

BETTER (D to C) At the next levels candidates will pay some attention to the specific question and start to make connected comment *with support from the text*. They will also choose their words more effectively. They may write along these lines:

EXAMINER'S SECRET
Quotations worked into your own writing are a neat and concise way of referring to the text. They can make your point in a way that longer, separate quotations often do not.

Ferlinghetti contrasts two couples, one rich one poor. The 'beautiful' couple in the car are like a pair of film stars, dressed in the latest fashion. The poet emphasises that they are 'elegant' like their Mercedes.

The garbagemen are described as 'grungy'. They wear 'red plastic blazers' but the man in the car wears an expensive suit. The poet goes on to say that the couple in the car are like people in a TV ad. I think Ferlinghetti is trying to say that they are not like real people and live in a fantasy world.

At the end Ferlinghetti shows that he is worried that rich and poor people can exist in a society like America.

In 'What Were They Like?' Denise Levertov asks us to think about the people of Vietnam. She thinks that Americans did not really know anything about the people they were fighting in the war. In her answers to the questions she shows that their way of life has been destroyed by the war. For example, when asked if they laughed, the answer is 'laughter is bitter to the burned mouth'.

Both poets are concerned with the underdog.

- This response is uneven but it contains some clear *comment* on the fashionable couple and tries to say something about how they *contrast* with the garbagemen through the clothes they wear.

- The candidate is also aware of how the couples are *presented* in the references to how poet 'emphasises' elegance and how the garbagemen are 'described' as grungy. The personal comment that the rich couple live in a fantasy world is also valid comment.

- By choosing Levertov's poem, the candidate is able to make a useful *cross-reference* in the claim that both poets are interested in the underdog. There is no direct support for this claim but what the candidate says about American attitudes and the effects of the war, show an *awareness* of the issues.

BEST (B to A*) The best candidates do not necessarily have to give an account of the poems' content. They assume the examiner has read the Anthology! They concentrate on comment and the authors' methods and achievements. They may write along these lines:

Ferlinghetti in 'Two Scavengers' and John Agard in 'Half-Caste' present people in very different ways. Ferlinghetti

EXAMINER'S SECRET

Remember that you cannot write about everything that can be said about a poem. Concentrate on the ideas most closely related to the question.

EXAMINER'S SECRET

Sometimes, when there is a range of similar features in a text you can give a couple of examples and use the simple device 'etc.' rather than trying to list everything.

looks on from the outside at people in a street, whilst Agard takes us into the mind of an individual. Yet both are concerned with injustice and how people are judged. Ferlinghetti exposes the shallowness of the 'cool couple' by describing them solely in terms of their appearance and possessions – the Mercedes, the linen suit, the 'casually coifed' hair, etc.

In particular, the sunglasses are a fashion icon that completes the image that could come out of 'some odorless TV ad'. In contrast the garbageman's sunglasses seem to represent a hopeless attempt to enter a forbidden world. The working people are ignored; they are 'grungy', 'scavengers'; they may look like 'some gargoyle Quasimodo' but society depends on them.

Agard too, is concerned with people's ignorance. Just as people like the garbagemen are lumped together as scavengers, Agard is concerned with the thoughtless attitude to people of mixed race. Unlike Ferlinghetti's clever but rather serious approach, Agard wittily pokes fun at people's attitudes and creates a portrait of a lively character who can even joke about the English weather: 'England weather nearly always half-caste'.

This is a much more complex approach.

- The choice of **'Half-Caste'** as second poem may seem unusual but it allows the candidate to make some very interesting points of comparison between external and internal ways of looking at people.

- There is no attempt to work through either poem line by line.

- The candidate marshals the references and quotations to reinforce *ideas*. From the start the candidate thinks about *how* the authors set about their tasks.

- The candidate *embeds* very *brief* quotations into the argument so as to *integrate* comment and example.

- The candidate draws together the wider issues raised by the poem and specific details.

- Most importantly, the candidate keeps to the subject of the question and writes about presentation.

Bear in mind these samples are only examples of different approaches. They are not complete answers.

SAMPLE ESSAY PLAN

Compare 'Presents from my Aunts in Pakistan' and *one* other poem and show how poets explore ideas about identity.

Opening key statement
- The arrival of clothes from another culture is used as a means of exploring a sense of divided identity.

- British clothes are seen as 'safe' (but boring), helping the girl to fit in.

Development
- The girl's divided feelings are implied in the way the clothes are described; the rich fabrics and colours sound very attractive.

Evaluation
- Her uncertain cultural identity is revealed in her reaction to wearing the clothes; she can't resist trying them on, but they make her feel uncomfortable and only emphasise that she is 'half-English' (line 25).

Another key idea
The second part of the poem deals with:

- Identity through a sense of place. In her imagination the girl creates a world she has never known. But even as she is imagining life in Lahore, she is reminded that she does not fit in there either; she is 'of no fixed nationality' (line 67) and only an onlooker.

 **EXAMINER'S SECRET**

A very brief quotation, often no more than a single word can make a very *precise* point. If you use long quotations, you are in effect asking the examiner to guess what key word(s) you have in mind.

 **EXAMINER'S SECRET**

Two of the most important words in your vocabulary should be 'but' and 'however'. Properly used, they can indicate your ability to connect ideas. We could also add words and phrases like 'nevertheless', 'on the other hand', 'whereas' 'in contrast', and 'even so'.

Wider issues

- The theft of her mother's jewellery seems to symbolise how her other culture has been taken away from her. (A woman's jewellery is an important expression of her status in India.)

- The aunts' request for cardigans bridges the gap between the two worlds, but does perhaps also make us question why they should want such mundane western garments.

Link to second poem

In comparison, **'What Were They Like?'** deals with the sense of identity, not just of an individual, but also of a whole people, whose identity seems to have been almost completely obliterated.

- This is suggested by the use of the past tense and words suggesting uncertainty etc., many of which are repeated.

- The question and answer format emphasises how little now seems to be known about these people.

Amplification

- There are two voices in the poem, both 'outsiders', though the 'questioner' is more detached than the answering voice – as shown in the difference in their language.

- The second half of the poem is much more descriptive and evocative. It is through this second voice that the message of the poem comes across.

Contrast and conclusion

- **'Presents from my Aunts in Pakistan'** offers a first person view of issues of identity, even though we may assume that the girl's experience is not unique.

- **'What Were They Like?'** seems to take a more detached view: 'It is not remembered' rather than 'I remember'.

- Despite this difference in approach, intense emotion lies behind both poems.

FURTHER QUESTIONS

1 Compare 'Vultures' with **one** other poem, showing how the poets explore the ideas about injustice.

2 Compare the ways in which the poets present ideas about rich and poor people in 'Two Scavengers in a Truck, Two Beautiful People in a Mercedes' and **one** other poem of your choice from this selection.

Write about:

● What rich and poor people are like

● What the poets think about rich and poor people

● How the poets use language to bring out the differences between rich and poor people

● Which poem you prefer and why

3 Compare (from) 'In Search For My Tongue' with **one** other poem, showing how poets bring out the importance of language in our lives.

4 Compare 'Limbo' with **one** other poem and show how the poets use the sounds of spoken English to present their ideas.

5 How do the poets use particular details to bring out their ideas in 'Vultures' and **one** other poem?

6 Compare 'Not My Business' with **one** other poem that has a moral, explaining how the poets reveal their feelings.

7 Compare the ways in which the poets present different environments in 'Night of the Scorpion' and **one** other poem of your choice from the selection.

Write about:

● What the environments are like

● Why the poets use the environments

● How the language brings out what the environments are like

8 Compare 'This Room' with **one** other poem and show how the poets explore the advantages and disadvantages of separate cultures.

EXAMINER'S SECRET
Examination questions are not designed to catch you out. They ask you to consider major, not obscure, aspects of the poems.

EXAMINER'S SECRET

When you have grasped the general format of the questions, it is often quite helpful to put yourself in the examiner's shoes and make up your own.

9 Compare the ways in which poems can express strong ideas and feelings about a subject in 'What Were They were Like?' and **one** other poem.

Write about:

● What their ideas are

● What their feelings are

● The methods they use to reveal their feelings

10 Compare 'Love After Love' with **one** other poem that takes an optimistic view of life. Examine the poets' ideas and how they present them.

Now take a break!

allusion (allude, alluding) a reference, often hidden or indirect, to words, ideas or other information. For example, in 'Love After Love', Derek Walcott seems to be *alluding* to the rituals of traditional hospitality, the celebration of the Christian Mass and possibly the Rubaiyat of Omar Khayam (see **Detailed summaries**). Of course, the full effect of allusion can be appreciated only if the reader recognises such un-stated connections

cliché a ready-made and overused expression or idea

conditional a grammatical term that is used of verbs such as 'could', 'should', 'would', etc., that suggest a degree of uncertainty, unlike positive forms like 'can', 'shall', 'will'

diction the particular vocabulary used by a poet

enjambment the effect created when two or more lines of verse run together continuously without any break at the end of the line. For example:

> '…Ten hours
> of steady rain hed driven him
> to crawl beneath a sack of rice.'

eye dialect the use of non-standard spelling to represent dialect forms or particular accents

irony (ironic, ironically) basically saying one thing but meaning another, it can take many forms. A situation may be ironic because it has a significance that may not be evident at the time or an expression may be ironic because it suggests meanings other than the literal sense. For example, we may ask whether in 'Two Scavengers' the couple in the Mercedes really are 'beautiful'

juxtapose (juxtaposition) to place together two or more, possibly contrasting, ideas

metaphor (metaphorical) the fusion of two different ideas so that one thing is likened to another. For example, in 'Search For My Tongue', the author's native language is likened to a plant: 'it blossoms out of my mouth'

monologue a narration or account delivered by a single voice

monosyllable (monosyllabic) a word of a single syllable. For example, the first line of 'Search for My Tongue' comprises six monosyllabic words: 'You ask me what I mean'

motif a repeated phrase or idea that acts like a symbol or emblem, for example, the word 'limbo' in the poem of the same name

oral tradition a body of literature and song that has been passed down from generation to generation by word of mouth

paradox (paradoxical) a seemingly contradictory statement or situation. For example, it seems paradoxical that ugly creatures, such as vultures that live off dead bodies, should show affection towards each other

persona an imagined character or role assumed by a writer, often the 'speaker' behind a poem's voice. For example, 'Limbo' is written in the first person but the words 'I' and 'me' do not refer to the poet, Edward Kamau Brathwaite, but to the persona he assumes, the transported African slave

polysyllable (polysyllabic) a word of more than one syllable, unlike a **monosyllable**

rhetoric (rhetorical) literally the art of persuasion, but a term used of any arrangement or patterning of words, such as repetition, that creates impressive effects above and beyond its literal meaning. Consider, for example, the repeated structures in 'Not My Business'

CHECKPOINT HINTS/ANSWERS

CHECKPOINT 1 Vultures

CHECKPOINT 2 They represent the invisible barrier between the rich and the poor.

CHECKPOINT 3 South Africa is officially a multi-cultural society. There is no racial segregation but there is economic segregation and for many people the effects are nearly the same.

CHECKPOINT 4 The repetition emphasises his struggle to wake up, and it is separated because it is not part of his dream.

CHECKPOINT 5 There is such a mass of bodies clamouring to collect the precious water that they seem to act like one.

CHECKPOINT 6 Their 'red plastic blazers' (line 4) are company issue, cheap and disposable. They contrast with the expensive 'three-piece linen suit' (line 1).

CHECKPOINT 7 A Mercedes is an easily-identifiable icon, or symbol, of wealth and superiority. The fact that it is an up-market foreign car and a convertible adds another layer of status and sophistication.

CHECKPOINT 8 The situation is highly charged and the sting could be fatal. The author takes a detached view and observes people's behaviour. His remark that the neighbours sat round doing nothing but wore 'the peace of understanding on each face' (line 31) seems almost sarcastic, as though, even as a young boy, he had no trust in their superstition.

CHECKPOINT 9 The scorpion is referred to as 'he' not 'it' as though it had human characteristics. On the other hand, the peasants who flock to the scene take on the characteristics of insects: they came 'like swarms of flies' (line 8), 'buzzed' (line 9), threw

'giant scorpion shadows' (line 12) and 'clicked' (line 15).

CHECKPOINT 10 This child's word for her father seems so out of place in the context of 'human roast' (line 33) but it draws attention to the close and affectionate relationship between the Commandant, who is responsible for so many deaths, and his child. It also provides a link with the vultures inclining 'affectionately' (line 12).

CHECKPOINT 11 'Killed', 'bitter', 'charred', 'burned', 'smashed up', 'scream'

CHECKPOINT 12 Moniza Alvi and Imtiaz Dhaker

CHECKPOINT 13 'would rot, rot and die in your mouth' (lines 12–13). Ironically the tongue 'dies' at this point but comes alive again later.

CHECKPOINT 14 Grace Nichols' 'Island Man'

CHECKPOINT 15 Apart from its literal meaning, having only 'one leg to stand on' is a conventional expression which suggests the speaker has a weak argument, and may have difficulty in defending his ideas – obviously not the case here!

CHECKPOINT 16 'another, who knows you by heart' (line 11). You have 'ignored' (line 10) this person (yourself – your 'true' self) who knows as much about you as if it had been deliberately studied ('by heart').

CHECKPOINT 17 'nightmares' (line 7), 'dark corners' (line 8), 'clouds' (line 9).

CHECKPOINT 18 She could be expressing breathless excitement. It has all happened so quickly that she hardly knows 'where I've left my feet' (she has been 'swept off her feet').
   OR
She is feeling disoriented, wondering how to 'find her feet' in a new world order, where she feels out of control – 'my hands are outside'.

CHECKPOINT 19 The victims are named but the authorities are simply a faceless 'they'.

CHECKPOINT 20
- 'salwar kameez' (line 1)
- 'embossed slippers' (line 5)
- 'glass bangles' (line 7)
- 'apple-green sari' (line 13)
- 'satin-silken top' (line 16)
- 'camel-skin lamp' (line 27)
- 'mirror-work' (line 44)
- 'fractured land' (line 58)
- 'shaded rooms' (line 61)
- 'screened from male visitors' (line 62)
- 'beggars' (line 65)
- 'sweeper-girls' (line 65)
- 'fretwork' (line 68)
- 'Shalimar Gardens' (line 69)

CHECKPOINT 21 They are essentially English and although they may appear ordinary to us they are appreciated as 'exotic' and desirable in Pakistan.

CHECKPOINT 22 The phrase 'Reaping havoc' is a paradox. The first word is productive; the second, destructive.

CHECKPOINT 23 Her heart is 'unchained' (line 27) and she asks the hurricane to 'break the frozen lake in me' (line 33).

CHECKPOINT 24 The downtown area of any American city is the central business area where wealth is concentrated.

TEST YOURSELF (CLUSTER 1)

1 Blessing

2 Limbo

3 Two Scavengers

4 What Were They Like?

5 Island Man

6 Nothing's Changed

7 Night of the Scorpion

8 Vultures

TEST YOURSELF (CLUSTER 2)

1 This Room

2 Hurricane Hits England

3 Not My Business

4 Presents from my Aunts in Pakistan

5 Search For My Tongue

6 Half-Caste

7 Love After Love

8 Unrelated Incidents

NOTES

Maya Angelou
I Know Why the Caged Bird Sings

Jane Austen
Pride and Prejudice

Alan Ayckbourn
Absent Friends

Elizabeth Barrett Browning
Selected Poems

Robert Bolt
A Man for All Seasons

Harold Brighouse
Hobson's Choice

Charlotte Brontë
Jane Eyre

Emily Brontë
Wuthering Heights

Shelagh Delaney
A Taste of Honey

Charles Dickens
David Copperfield
Great Expectations
Hard Times
Oliver Twist

Roddy Doyle
Paddy Clarke Ha Ha Ha

George Eliot
Silas Marner
The Mill on the Floss

Anne Frank
The Diary of a Young Girl

William Golding
Lord of the Flies

Oliver Goldsmith
She Stoops to Conquer

Willis Hall
The Long and the Short and the Tall

Thomas Hardy
Far from the Madding Crowd

The Mayor of Casterbridge
Tess of the d'Urbervilles
The Withered Arm and other Wessex Tales

L.P. Hartley
The Go-Between

Seamus Heaney
Selected Poems

Susan Hill
I'm the King of the Castle

Barry Hines
A Kestrel for a Knave

Louise Lawrence
Children of the Dust

Harper Lee
To Kill a Mockingbird

Laurie Lee
Cider with Rosie

Arthur Miller
The Crucible
A View from the Bridge

Robert O'Brien
Z for Zachariah

Frank O'Connor
My Oedipus Complex and Other Stories

George Orwell
Animal Farm

J.B. Priestley
An Inspector Calls
When We Are Married

Willy Russell
Educating Rita
Our Day Out

J.D. Salinger
The Catcher in the Rye

William Shakespeare
Henry IV Part I
Henry V
Julius Caesar

Macbeth
The Merchant of Venice
A Midsummer Night's Dream
Much Ado About Nothing
Romeo and Juliet
The Tempest
Twelfth Night

George Bernard Shaw
Pygmalion

Mary Shelley
Frankenstein

R.C. Sherriff
Journey's End

Rukshana Smith
Salt on the snow

John Steinbeck
Of Mice and Men

Robert Louis Stevenson
Dr Jekyll and Mr Hyde

Jonathan Swift
Gulliver's Travels

Robert Swindells
Daz 4 Zoe

Mildred D. Taylor
Roll of Thunder, Hear My Cry

Mark Twain
Huckleberry Finn

James Watson
Talking in Whispers

Edith Wharton
Ethan Frome

William Wordsworth
Selected Poems

A Choice of Poets

Mystery Stories of the Nineteenth Century including The Signalman

Nineteenth Century Short Stories

Poetry of the First World War

Six Women Poets

Margaret Atwood
Cat's Eye
The Handmaid's Tale

Jane Austen
Emma
Mansfield Park
Persuasion
Pride and Prejudice
Sense and Sensibility

Alan Bennett
Talking Heads

William Blake
Songs of Innocence and of Experience

Charlotte Brontë
Jane Eyre
Villette

Emily Brontë
Wuthering Heights

Angela Carter
Nights at the Circus

Geoffrey Chaucer
The Franklin's Prologue and Tale
The Miller's Prologue and Tale
The Prologue to the Canterbury Tales
The Wife of Bath's Prologue and Tale

Samuel Coleridge
Selected Poems

Joseph Conrad
Heart of Darkness

Daniel Defoe
Moll Flanders

Charles Dickens
Bleak House
Great Expectations
Hard Times

Emily Dickinson
Selected Poems

John Donne
Selected Poems

Carol Ann Duffy
Selected Poems

George Eliot
Middlemarch
The Mill on the Floss

T.S. Eliot
Selected Poems
The Waste Land

F. Scott Fitzgerald
The Great Gatsby

E.M. Forster
A Passage to India

Brian Friel
Translations

Thomas Hardy
Jude the Obscure
The Mayor of Casterbridge
The Return of the Native
Selected Poems
Tess of the d'Urbervilles

Seamus Heaney
Selected Poems from 'Opened Ground'

Nathaniel Hawthorne
The Scarlet Letter

Homer
The Iliad
The Odyssey

Aldous Huxley
Brave New World

Kazuo Ishiguro
The Remains of the Day

Ben Jonson
The Alchemist

James Joyce
Dubliners

John Keats
Selected Poems

Christopher Marlowe
Doctor Faustus
Edward II

Arthur Miller
Death of a Salesman

John Milton
Paradise Lost Books I & II

Toni Morrison
Beloved

George Orwell
Nineteen Eighty-Four

Sylvia Plath
Selected Poems

Alexander Pope
Rape of the Lock & Selected Poems

William Shakespeare
Antony and Cleopatra
As You Like It
Hamlet
Henry IV Part I
King Lear
Macbeth
Measure for Measure
The Merchant of Venice
A Midsummer Night's Dream
Much Ado About Nothing
Othello
Richard II
Richard III
Romeo and Juliet
The Taming of the Shrew
The Tempest
Twelfth Night
The Winter's Tale

George Bernard Shaw
Saint Joan

Mary Shelley
Frankenstein

Jonathan Swift
Gulliver's Travels and A Modest Proposal

Alfred Tennyson
Selected Poems

Virgil
The Aeneid

Alice Walker
The Color Purple

Oscar Wilde
The Importance of Being Earnest

Tennessee Williams
A Streetcar Named Desire

Jeanette Winterson
Oranges Are Not the Only Fruit

John Webster
The Duchess of Malfi

Virginia Woolf
To the Lighthouse

W.B. Yeats
Selected Poems
Metaphysical Poets